I0798624

SHARING THROUGH SONG

I WILL FOLLOW GOD'S PLAN FOR ME

VOLUME ONE

SHARING THROUGH SONG

I WILL FOLLOW GOD'S PLAN FOR ME

VOLUME ONE

BY

ALISON PALMER

Horizon Publishers
Springville, Utah

ISBN: 0-88290-780-8
v.1

Published by Horizon Publishers
an imprint of Cedar Fort, Inc.
925 N. Main Springville, Ut., 84663
www.cedarfort.com

Distributed by:

Cover design by Nicole Williams

Printed in the United States of America
10 9 8 7 6 5 4 3 2 1

Printed on acid-free paper

Acknowledgments

Many thanks are extended to Duane S. Crowther, president and senior editor of Horizon Publishers, for continuing to walk the path of faith with me and preparing my manuscript for publication.

Thanks, as well, to Debra Stinson for her dedication and hard work creating beautiful illustrations from my pathetic sketches and vague descriptions.

I also need to express my gratitude for my husband for patiently reminding me that reaching for the stars only leads to burns, but pursuing something that makes you happy truly can lead to joy. Though I can't do and be all that I'd like, he gives me the freedom to do what makes me happy. Thank you for your patience and understanding.

Thankfulness and love are also expressed to my children, for cheerfully eating cold cereal for dinner more times than I'd care to admit, as I worked to complete the book.

Most of all, I must express my love and gratitude toward my Heavenly Father. He continues to bless me, even when it has been undeserved. He filled my soul with the thoughts and ideas that became this book. May the lives of many children be blessed through His inspiration.

INTRODUCTION

Dear Friends,

Some years ago, as a Primary chorister, I was kindly told that I needed to teach the children differently than I had always done. It seemed that the Lord's program was somewhat different from my program. After much research, and even more prayer, I determined that changes were in harmony with the Lord's way and I needed to try my best to serve Him as He had asked me to.

Sharing time and singing time are not separate entities, as most of us would have them. We have been asked by the General Primary Board to use a full 30–40 minutes for sharing time: in which time, music is integrated throughout. (See "Instructions for Sharing Time," *2005 Outline for Sharing Time and the Children's Sacrament Meeting Presentation*, p. 1.) This is not always easy. Compliance requires early preparation and more communication and cooperation between presidencies and choristers, but it works.

Music teaches where words fail and if we do not merge the two, we are missing beautiful opportunities to teach our children things they will always remember.

This manual is designed for those who are valiantly trying to change, as I needed to. This does not, however, limit its possibilities. Please feel free to mold these lessons to fit your needs as a leader, teacher or parent.

Please also keep in mind that this is copyrighted material, intended for use within the purchaser's home or Primary unit only. If you enjoy using it, share that information with your friends, but allow them to show honesty by purchasing their own copy of this manual.

May the Lord bless you in your endeavors to serve His children.

Sincerely,
Alison Palmer

Contents

1. I Will Follow God's Plan

Children's Songbook p. 164

Opening Song: **I Am a Child of God** *Children's Songbook* p. 2

Closing Song: **I Will Follow God's Plan** *Children's Songbook* p. 164

Materials Needed

- Small display table
- 2 Large cloth coverings for the table
- Small gift box
- Road map
- Picture of the Premortal existence (may use the *2005 Outline for Sharing Time and the Children's Sacrament Presentation*)
- Small globe, or picture of the earth (*Gospel Art Picture* #600)
- One set of scriptures
- Hammer
- Binoculars
- Figurine of a child praying, or picture (available in **Ten Commandments** lesson)
- One tennis shoe
- Copy of one smiley face from **My Gospel Standards** lesson

Preparation

- Drape one cloth over the table so that it touches the floor in front and covers as much of the two sides as possible.
- Place the materials on the display table. The other cloth will be used to cover the items from the children's view.

Teaching Suggestions

Tell the children that the items on the table represent different things they will be learning about in the coming year. These same things are also the words to the first new song that they will learn. Share the name of the song and ask them what they think it means. Allow them to give their thoughts.

Bear testimony to the children that Heavenly Father loves them; He knows them individually and has prepared a way for them to be happy and to return to Him again. Emphasize the importance of learning Heavenly Father's plan because we love Him as well. Briefly testify of the happiness living the gospel has brought into your own life.

Show the children the items on your table: in order of mention in the song. Repeat the corresponding words with the children, and then briefly explain what each topic will focus on as quoted below from the *2005 Outline for Sharing Time and the Children's Sacrament Meeting Presentation.*

Stop after every couple of items to review the words learned to that point, always referencing them to the visual item from your table. Then, sing the song to that point. Repeat the process until the children have become comfortable with the general concepts of the song and all the words have been practiced.

Note that there is no visual for the words "I will follow God's plan for me." Point out to the children that they are who the song talks about. Allow the children to point to themselves, or stand at their seat, during this portion of the song.

The next step is to cover the display table and remove a random item without the children seeing. Hide the removed item on the floor under your table drape. Show the table again and ask the children what is missing. Help them identify the item and remind them of the words it represented.

Tell them that since the item is missing they must hum those words when they come in the song. Sing the song, inserting humming at the appropriate point. It helps to have the pianist enter a small pause just before the missing phrase and a small pause when singing should begin again. Return the missing object to the table and repeat the memory game with the remaining time.

Close with a brief reminder of your testimony and how happy you are to be sharing this knowledge with the children.

Words and Corresponding Items

- *My life is a gift;* (Gift box) "I am grateful for the gift of eternal life."
- *My life has a plan.* (Road map) "I came to earth to receive a body and be tested."
- *My life has a purpose; in heav'n it began.* (Picture of the Premortal existence) "Heavenly Father presented His plan for us in the Grand Council in Heaven. We were all there and chose to follow His plan."
- *My choice was to come to this lovely home on earth* (Small globe) "As part of Heavenly Father's plan the earth was created."
- *And seek for God's light to direct me from birth.* (Binoculars) "As I pray and study the scriptures, I learn what Heavenly Father wants me to do."
- *Holding fast to his word and his love.* (Scriptures) "I learn about Jesus Christ as I read the scriptures. My faith grows as I learn about Him."
- *I will work,* (Hammer) "I share the gospel as I serve others."
- *I will pray;* (Child praying) "I can pray to Heavenly Father and receive answers to my prayers."
- *I will always walk in his way.* (Tennis shoe) Jesus Christ taught the gospel and set the example by the way He lived."
- *Then I will be happy on earth—And in my home above.* (Smiley face) "I am grateful for Heavenly Father's plan. It teaches me how to be happy."

2. THE PLAN OF SALVATION

Opening Song: **I Lived in Heaven** *Children's Songbook* p. 4

Closing Song: **I Will Follow God's Plan for Me** *Children's Songbook* p. 164

MATERIALS NEEDED

- Copy of questions and songs
- Container to hold questions and songs
- Copy of game board on an 11x17 paper. Or, use a projector or copier to make a larger image, assemble pieces onto butcher paper or poster board. It may also be drawn free-hand on the chalkboard.
- Chalkboard
- Two magnets to use as playing pieces (most meeting house chalkboards are magnetized) or other type of marker that can be affixed to the game board
- Tape

PREPARATION

- Mount game board on the chalkboard or other flat surface.
- Cut the questions and songs into individual strips; place these inside your container.

TEACHING SUGGESTIONS

Briefly review the Plan of Salvation, using the symbols on the game board.

Divide the children into two teams. Children must answer questions, and sing songs to move forward in the game. Correct answers or songs move the marker forward one section. Wrong answers stay in the same place.

The only exception is when the marker is in the premortal existence at "choice." If a wrong answer is given the marker is moved to "outer darkness." A right answer must then be provided on the next turn to be able to return to the right path. A right answer or song while on "choice" advances to "the veil" and by-passes "outer darkness."

QUESTIONS

- Name one reason we needed to come to earth.
- Where were we before we came to earth?
- What does Heavenly Father want us to do while we are on earth?
- Why did Jesus come to earth?
- What are the names of the three degrees of glory we can achieve after we die?
- Was Satan in the premortal existence with us?
- What does "Agency" mean?
- Who will be with us if we inherit the Celestial Kingdom?
- Where must we go if want to be able to go to the Celestial Kingdom?
- Where did Adam and Eve first live?
- What can I do to show Heavenly Father that I love him?
- What happens to our spirits and bodies when we die?
- What happens to our spirits and bodies during the Resurrection?
- Name one way we can learn what Heavenly Father wants us to do?
- What do we do each Sunday that helps us remember Jesus' sacrifice for us?

SONGS

- **I Am a Child of God** *Children's Songbook* p. 2
- **On a Golden Spring Time** *Children's Songbook* p. 88
- **I Love to See the Temple** *Children's Songbook* p. 95
- **I Like My Birthdays** *Children's Songbook* p. 104
- **Seek the Lord Early** *Children's Songbook* p. 108
- **Keep the Commandments** *Children's Songbook* p. 146
- **I Will Follow God's Plan** *Children's Songbook* p. 164
- **My Heavenly Father Loves Me** *Children's Songbook* p. 228
- **Because God Loves Me** *Children's Songbook* p. 234

The Plan of Salvation

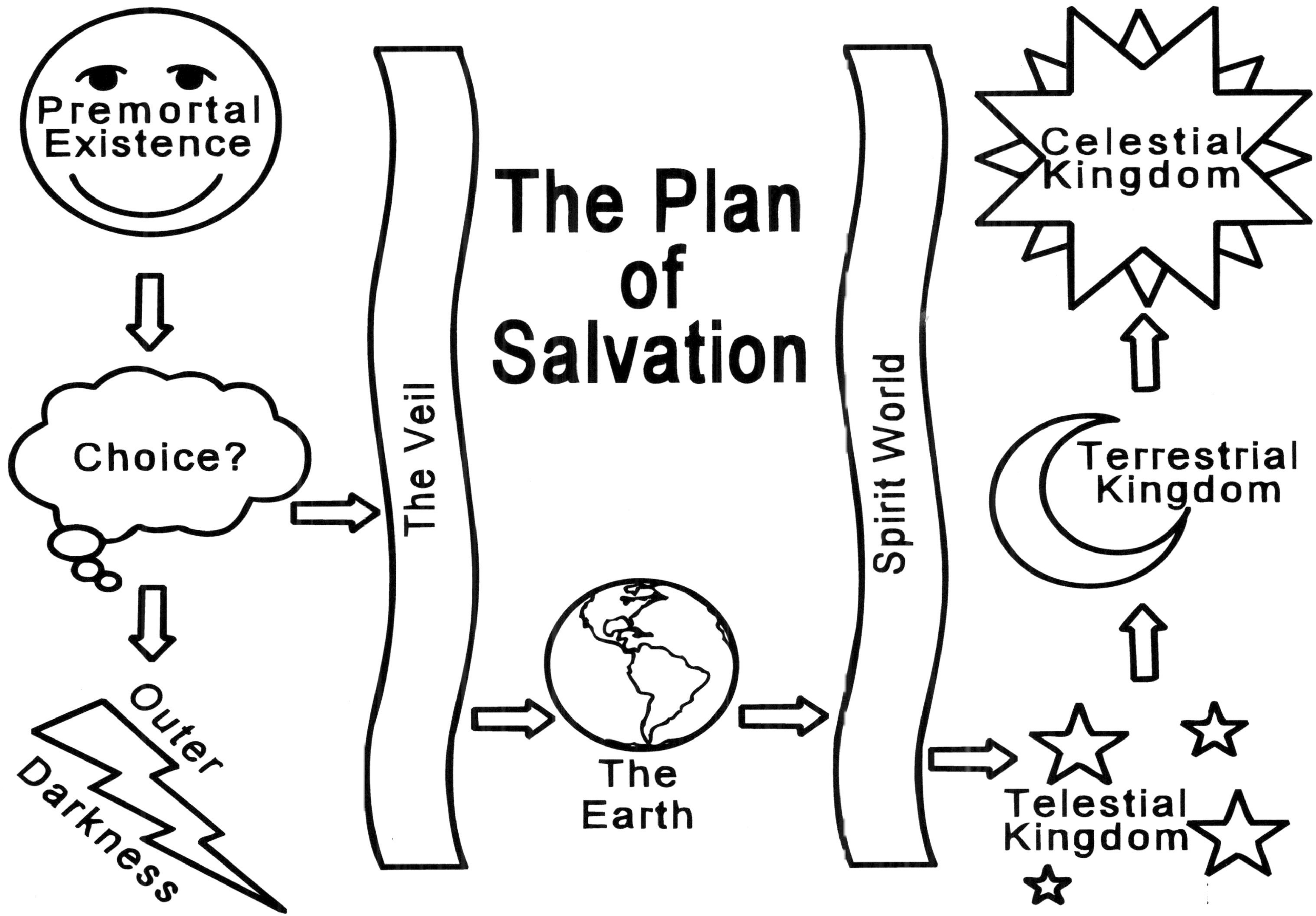

3. A CHILD'S PRAYER

Children's Songbook p. 12

Opening Song: **I Pray in Faith** *Children's Songbook* p. 14

Closing Song: **A Child's Prayer** *Children's Songbook* p. 12

MATERIALS NEEDED

- Chalk and chalkboard
- *Gospel Art Picture* #216 Christ and the Children

PREPARATION

- Write the words from **List 1** down the left side of the chalkboard.
- Write the words from **List 2** down the right side of the chalkboard in a random order.
- Be familiar with the message found in Matthew 19:13–14.

TEACHING SUGGESTIONS

Ask the children to pretend that they have friend who is just learning about the gospel. He has never prayed before and wonders what it's like. He wonders what to say and how it will feel. He wonders how he will know if Heavenly Father is even listening. Sometimes his parents don't seem to be listening to him, so why would Heavenly Father?

Ask them to share their thoughts about what they could say to this friend. This could include the steps of prayer, the language, the feelings, and the children's own convictions that Heavenly Father does love them, and that He listens.

Share your own testimony of these elements as well. Use the picture of Christ with the children to help illustrate your message.

The song they will be learning deals with a child who is also learning about prayer. He has questions, but he also learns the answers and learns that he loves to pray. Share the entire first verse with the children. The children will help their friend learn about prayer by matching the words from the first list to the corresponding words on second list. Tell them to listen carefully while you share the message again phrase by phrase. Then, have a child come up to draw a line from the key words on the first list to its matching phrase on the other side.

Always start at the beginning of the verse after a match is made. This provides repeated exposure to the words in the song. Stop after the first verse and introduce its melody on the piano. Have the children try to sing along.

Repeat the process with the second verse.

If time remains, try having the children sing along with the accompaniment.

WORD MATCH LISTS

	LIST 1	LIST 2
Verse 1	Heavenly Father	Really There
	Do You Hear	And Answer
	Heaven	Far Away
	I Feel It	Close Around Me
	Heavenly Father	I Remember
	Jesus Told	Long Ago
	Suffer	Come To Me
	Father, In Prayer	Now To Thee
Verse 2	Pray	Is There
	Speak	Is Listening
	You	His Child
	His Love	Surrounds You
	He Hears	Your Prayer
	He Loves	The Children
	Of Such	The Kingdom
	Kingdom	Of Heav'n

SPECIAL NOTES

- Save learning to sing both verses at the same time for another day. This can be done by just using the melody on the first two rounds, and then adding accompaniment for the third time only. This gives them a strong practice run to start with. It also helps to have more than one leader available to lead the separate groups.
- Singers may be divided so that the first and second verses are sung by different groups. Possible groupings include girls then boys, Junior Primary then Senior Primary, or children and then their teachers.
- This song is also beautiful without the accompaniment. The children may learn to sing the combined verses without the piano.
- You may also choose to use other instruments to help the children follow their melody lines. A flute for the first verse, a violin for the second, both on their respective verses for the combined verse.

4. The Second Article of Faith

Opening Song: **I Lived in Heaven** *Children's Songbook* p. 4

Closing Song: **The Second Article of Faith** *Children's Songbook* p. 122

Materials Needed

- Copy of the included illustrations on cardstock
- Chalkboard or other area for display of the choices
- Flannel board for display of story pieces
- Flannel or hook tape
- Tape
- 20 index cards
- Yarn
- Hole punch
- Copy of the *Articles of Faith*

Preparation

- Be familiar with the story found in Moses 4.
- Color and cut out the illustrations. Back each piece with flannel or a piece of hook tape.
- Write the choices and consequences listed below on the index cards, or make up your own situations that you feel are appropriate for your Primary.
- Use the hole punch to place a hole in the left side of the choice cards, and the right side of the consequence cards.
- Cut 10 pieces of yarn about 2 yards long (slightly longer than the width of the area you are using for display).
- Tie one end of a piece of yarn to each choice card and the other end to its corresponding consequence card.
- Tape the choice cards onto the left side of the chalkboard with the words turned toward the board.

- Tape the consequence cards randomly on the right side of the board, hiding the words and creating a "tangled" pattern with the yarn.

Teaching Suggestions

Assemble the picture of the Garden of Eden while you briefly review the story of Adam and the fall. You may choose to pass out the pieces and let the children help you tell and put together the story.

As you tell the story, remind the children that the garden was a perfect place to live and that everything was provided for Adam and Eve.

Adam and Eve had a choice to make. They knew why they had been sent to earth and they knew the rules Heavenly Father had given them. Did the rules allow them to do everything that they were to do? Allow the children to express their own opinions on what their own choices would have been.

Because of the choices Adam and Eve made, we have agency today to make lots of choices. But, Adam did break a rule to give us this gift. What happened to him because he broke a rule? What happens to each of us if we break a rule? Would it be fair for us to be punished for something we didn't do?

Read the Second Article of Faith to the children. Ask them to repeat the words with you, and then share their views on what they think the statement means. Correct any misconceptions they might have.

Each of us needs to learn to take responsibility for our own actions. We are here to learn and grow, and part of that is making mistakes and repenting. Part of it is also doing things right and being blessed for it. Each of us must do this for ourselves. It wouldn't be fair if we had to repent because our neighbor was mean to his dog. It also wouldn't be fair if everyone got to go to the temple because their bishop was worthy, not them.

Show the children the choice cards. They will be pretending to make choices. Some choices may be right, some are wrong, each one has a consequence.

Pick a reverent child to come up and choose a card from the left side of the board. Read the situation. They must then follow the path of their string to find the consequence card and read the results of the "choice." Discuss if the choice was good or bad, and how it could be corrected, if need be. Then sing the corresponding song.

Choices, Consequences and Corresponding Songs

- **Choice**—Father asked you to clean out the garage before he gets home from work and you do it.
  Consequence—He was looking for the target for your bow and arrow set. Since you cleaned out the garage, he was able to find it and you can practice together. **Quickly I'll Obey** *Children's Songbook* p. 197.
- **Choice**—You decided you didn't want to go to church today.
  Consequence—Your friend called later to tell you about the story your teacher told during the lesson. You were sorry you missed it. **When I Go to Church** *Children's Songbook* p. 157.
- **Choice**—You didn't read your scriptures this week.
  Consequence—When a friend tries to tempt you to do something you shouldn't, you find it is harder to say "no" than it should be. **Seek the Lord Early** *Children's Songbook* p. 109.
- **Choice**—If you pay your tithing you won't have enough money to buy the new CD you want, but you pay it anyway.

Consequence—You find the CD on sale and get to buy it for less than you thought. **I Want to Give the Lord My Tenth** *Children's Songbook* p. 150.

- **Choice**—Your mom asks you to take treats to the new family on your street and you go.
  Consequence—You discover that they have a child just your age. **Friends Are Fun** *Children's Songbook* p. 262.
- **Choice**—You found some money in the hall at school. You decided to keep it.
  Consequence—Now you're spending all your time worrying about getting caught and somebody wanting their money back. **I Believe in Being Honest** *Children's Songbook* p. 149.
- **Choice**—You decide to play with you little brother, even though he's always a pain.
  Consequence—It seems that since you took time to play with him, he doesn't bug you as much. **A Happy Family** *Children's Songbook* p. 198.
- **Choice**—You buy a shirt that is a little immodest, but if you hold your arms right no one can tell.
  Consequence—Now you have to worry about what you're doing while you wear that shirt. **The Lord Gave Me a Temple** *Children's Songbook* p. 153.

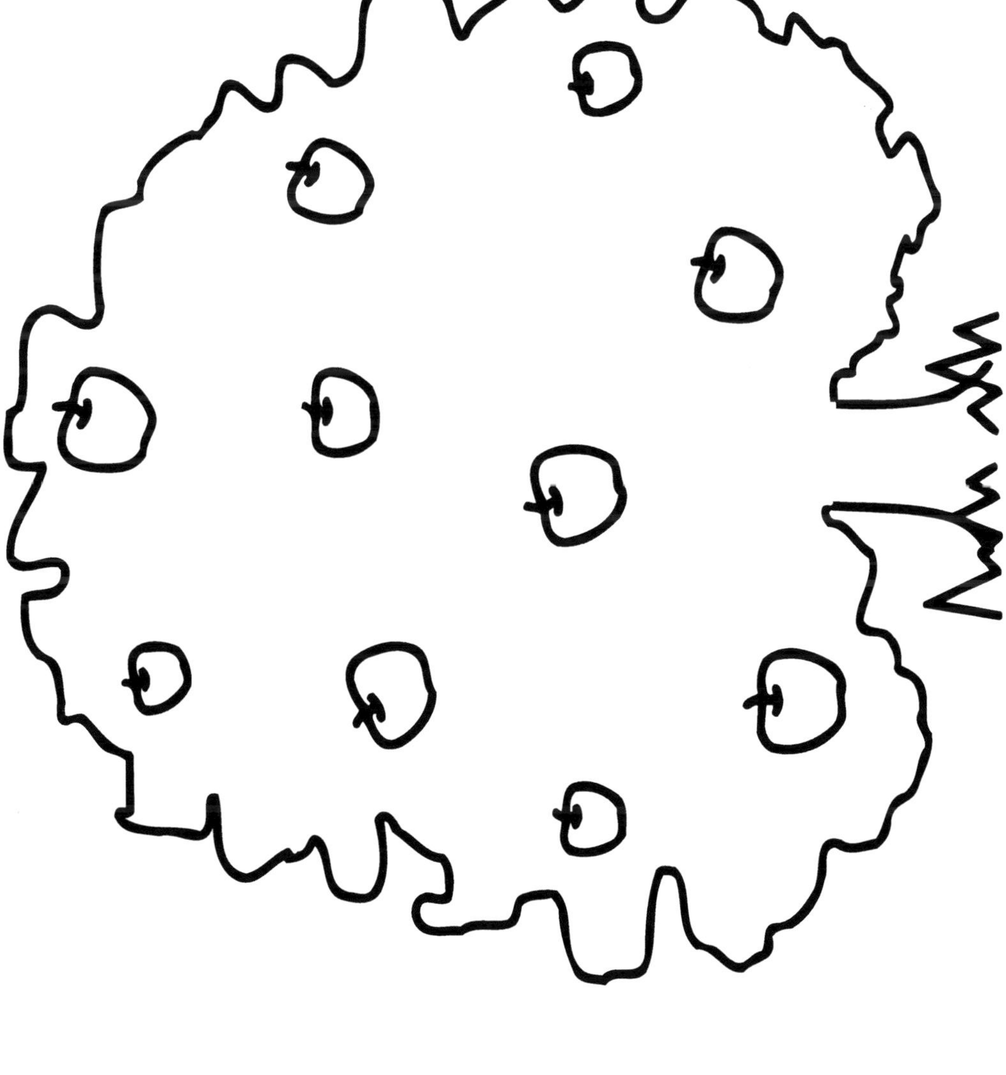

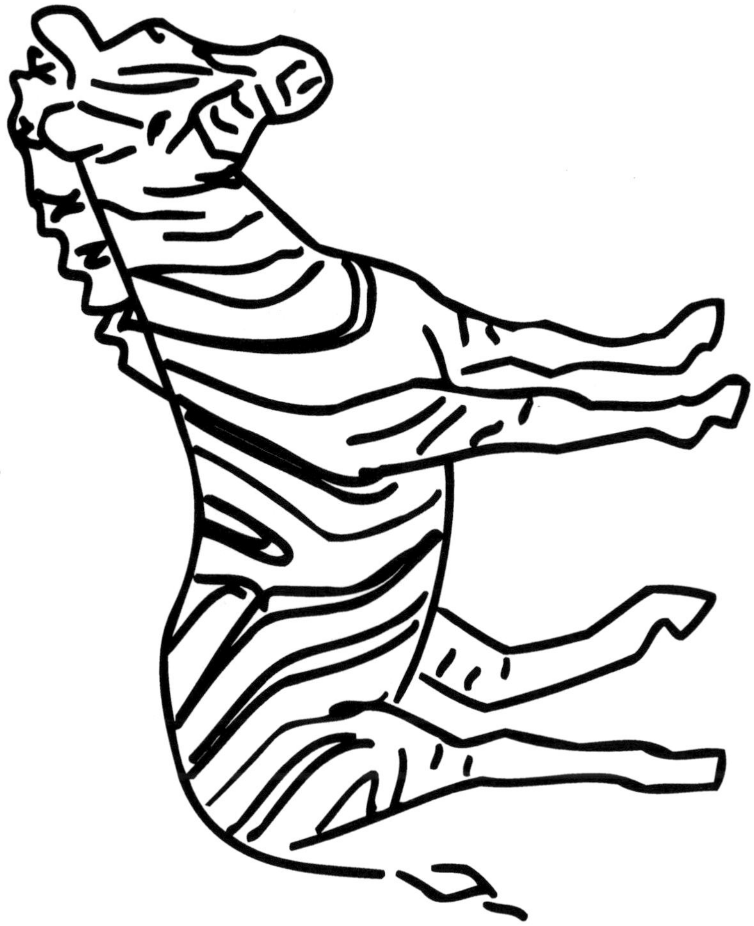

5. I Believe in Christ

Hymns #134

Opening Song: **Beautiful Savior** *Children's Songbook* p. 62

Closing Song: **I Believe in Christ** *Hymns* #134

Materials Needed

- Large picture of Christ

Preparation

- Invite individual classes to learn verses 2, 3, and 4. They should also find a picture to represent something in their verse and prepare a short message about the meaning of the words in their assigned verse.
- Become familiar with the included sign language gestures for this song. Please note that all words are not included and should not be signed. Those who communicate through sign language are not necessarily concerned with using correct grammar. Sign language is a beautiful expression of thoughts and ideas.
- Place the picture of Christ in a central area at the front of the room.

Teaching Suggestions

Begin with the class presentations of verses 2–4. Let each class stand when it is their turn, tell about the message of their verse and show their chosen picture, then have them sing.

Thank the children for their presentations and take special note of the feelings that are present. Share a brief portion of your testimony of the Savior with the children. Express that it is sometimes difficult to put our feelings for Christ into words.

Those things that we feel about Jesus Christ should also show in our actions. If we love Him, we will try to be like Him. They will learn the first verse of the song by learning to show some of the words in their actions. They will do this through sign language.

Start at the beginning and work with each phrase. Sing the phrase, show the corresponding signs while saying the words, practice the words and signs with the children, and then try the signs while singing. Practice the words and signs for each phrase independently, but sing the song as a whole to the point learned.

SPECIAL NOTE

- Consider performing this song as it was learned. Have the entire Primary sing the first verse and the individual classes sing their assigned verses. Then, repeat the first verse with all the children (or congregation and children) while the children sign the words.

I, Me

(point to self)

Believe

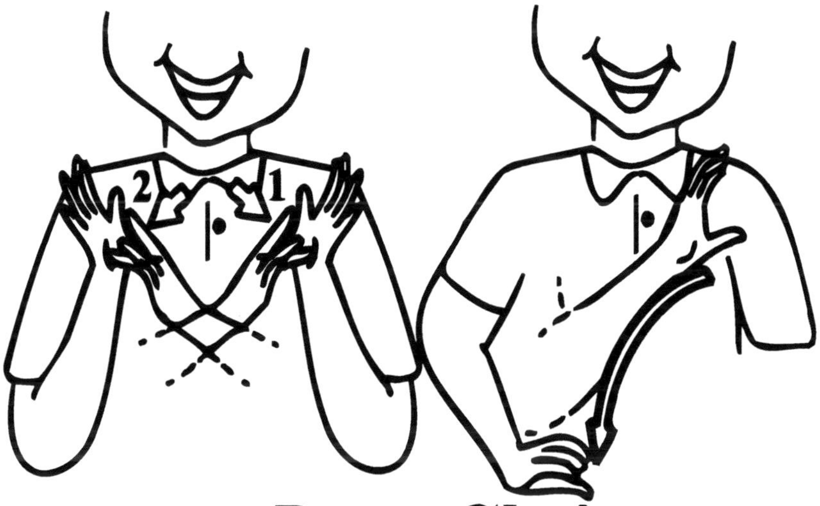

Jesus Christ

He, Him

(Christ)

(point to Heaven)

King

Heart

Sing

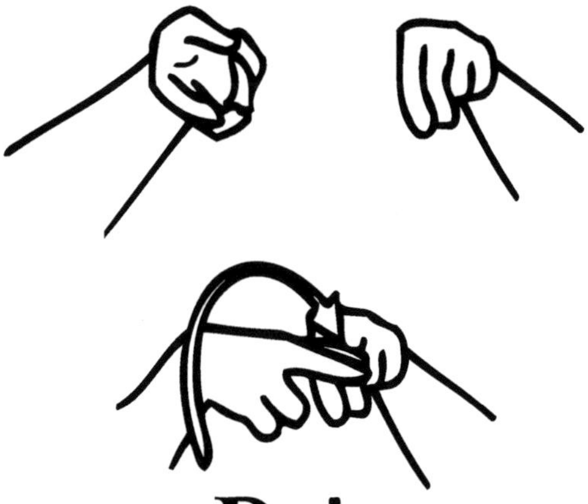

Raise

Voice,
Tongue Employ

Praise, Good

Joy

Grand

Amen

God's Own Son

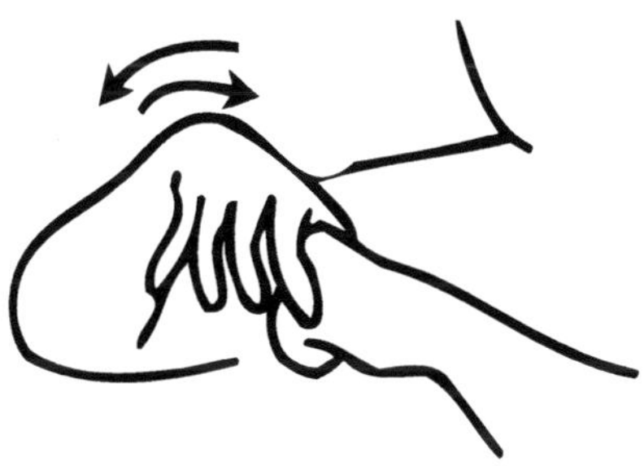

Earth

Dwell

Soul

Come

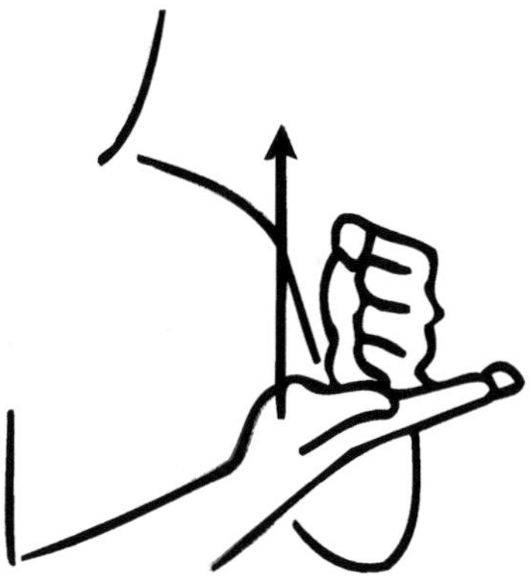

Healed

Sick

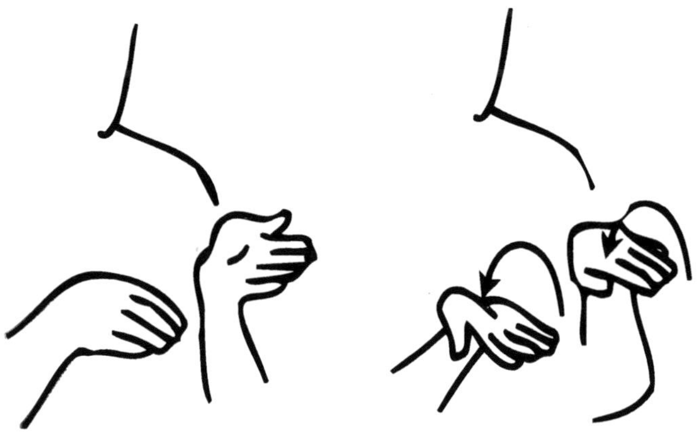

Dead

Work

Name

6. Jesus Atoned for Our Sins

Opening Song: **I Believe in Christ** *Hymns* #134

Closing Song: **To Think about Jesus** *Children's Songbook* p. 71

Materials Needed

- Color copies of *Gospel Art Pictures* #225–228, 230–231, and 234
- 7 Resealable plastic bags
- 7 Pieces of construction paper
- 7 Glue sticks
- Chalkboard or other flat surface for posting completed pictures
- Tape or appropriate fasteners

Note: If your Primary holds separate singing times, you will need to double the copies of each picture and construction paper.

Preparation

- Cut the copies of the pictures of Christ into large puzzle pieces. Make six to ten puzzle pieces per picture.
- Secure each puzzle separately in the plastic bags.

Teaching Suggestions

Divide the children into seven groups and give each a picture puzzle to put together. When they have figured out where each of the pieces fits, they should glue the pieces into place on the construction paper.

After all the children have finished assembling the puzzles, have them bring the pictures to the front and place them in order of occurrence. Then, invite the groups who completed each picture to come up in the correct order to briefly tell about the story their picture represents. As each group finishes their presentation, sing the corresponding song from the *Children's Songbook.*

When all the pictures have been presented and sung about, close with your testimony of the Savior, the atonement and resurrection.

PICTURES AND SONGS

- #225 The Last Supper: **The Sacrament** *Children's Songbook* p. 72
- #226 Jesus Washing the Apostles' Feet: **Love One Another** *Children's Songbook* pg. 136
- #227 Jesus Praying in Gethsemane: **A Child's Prayer** *Children's Songbook* p. 12
- #228 The Betrayal of Jesus: **I'm Trying to Be like Jesus** *Children's Songbook* p. 78
- #230 The Crucifixion: **Help Me Dear Father** *Children's Songbook* p. 99
- #231 Burial of Jesus: **He Died That We Might Live Again** *Children's Songbook* p. 65
- #234 Jesus Shows His Wounds: **He Sent His Son** *Children's Songbook* p. 34

7. Teach Me to Walk in the Light

Children's Songbook p. 177

Opening Song: **I Will Follow God's Plan** *Children's Songbook* p. 164

Closing Song: **Teach Me to Walk in the Light** *Children's Songbook* p. 177

Materials Needed

- Chalkboard
- Chalk
- 10 Copies of the light bulbs illustration
- Tape
- Working flashlight
- Blindfold
- Holy Bible

Preparation

- Cut out the light bulbs (color if desired).
- Tape the light bulbs on the side of the chalkboard.
- Write the words to **Teach Me to Walk in the Light** on the chalkboard in three columns, divided by verse.

Teaching Suggestions

Ask a child to come to the front of the room. Place the blindfold over his eyes, and then ask him to walk to the back of the room and touch the wall. Instruct the other children that they must be as quiet as they can and not interfere with the blindfolded child's journey.

Commend the child for his efforts and ask him how he felt about making the journey without being able to see. Then, ask him to make the journey to the front, blindfolded, but also holding the hand of a teacher or leader.

Read Ephesians 5:8 with the children.

Explain that Heavenly Father wants us to find light while we are on earth. Spiritual light represents the true gospel and the things Heavenly Father wants us to do to be happy and return to Him. Ask the children to name some things that can bring spiritual light into their lives, and allow them to share their thoughts. Remind the children that Heavenly Father has blessed them with parents and leaders who can help them find their way toward that light.

Show the words to the song. Explain that this song has three parts. The first verse is a child's prayer to Heavenly Father. The child is asking to know about Heavenly Father and how to walk in His light. The second verse uses a parent or leader, telling the child that she will walk with him and show him the light. The third verse is the parent and child walking together, sharing gratitude for being able to learn to be like Heavenly Father.

Next, show the children your flashlight. Explain that you will use the light to point to each word so they can follow along and learn to sing this song. Shine the light on the first line, say the words, and then trace the words with the light again as the children repeat them back to you. Continue through the verse in this manner. Stop every couple of lines to try the words learned to that point with accompaniment.

When all the words to a verse have been rehearsed, choose a reverent child to come up and be in charge of pointing to the words with the flashlight beam while the entire verse is sung.

When all three verses have been sung separately, ask the children to name words that they remember singing a lot (teach, walk, and light). Cover all the places in the song where those words occur, and then try singing the song again.

If time remains, have children suggest ways that families help us live the gospel and return to Heavenly Father. For each suggestion, the child may choose a word to cover up in the song. Repeat the song after every two or three words are covered.

End with your testimony of gratitude for being able to learn that Heavenly Father loves us and that He has given us families and teachers that can help us get back to Him.

SPECIAL NOTES

This song is easily performed in several ways.

- All of the children can sing all three verses.
- The children can be divided by Junior and Senior Primary; the younger children sing verse one, the older sing verse two, verse three is sung together.
- The entire Primary sings verse one, the congregation (or the Primary leaders and teachers) verse two, and together again on three.
- Soloists may also be considered.

8. FAMILY PROCLAMATION

Opening Song: **Teach Me to Walk in the Light** *Children's Songbook* p. 177

Closing Song: **Love Is Spoken Here** *Children's Songbook* p. 190

MATERIALS NEEDED

- Copies of *The Family: A Proclamation to the World* for each class
- Dress-up clothes to represent different members of a family: Father, Mother, a Young Child, Brother, Sister and Teenagers
- *Children's Songbooks* for reference by the classes
- Copy of the family situations
- Small container to hold situations

PREPARATION

- Cut apart the family situations and place them into the container.
- Prayerfully read *The Family: A Proclamation to the World* and decide which portions are most important for your children to read and discuss with you.

TEACHING SUGGESTIONS

Discuss how and why the First Presidency issued the proclamation. The proclamation is to help us understand what God expects of us as members of a family and why families are important.

Have the children help you read small portions of the proclamation aloud. Help the children understand the meanings and explain any words that appear difficult for them. End with the middle of the seventh paragraph.

"Happiness in family life is most likely to be achieved when founded upon the teachings of the Lord Jesus Christ. Successful marriages and families are established and maintained on principles of faith, prayer, repentance, forgiveness, respect, love, compassion, work, and wholesome recreational activities." (*The Family: A Proclamation To The World,* 1995)

Have the teachers draw a situation from the container for their class to discuss and work out a solution. Class members must then dress-up and briefly role-play the situation's righteous solution for the rest of Primary. They must also choose a Primary song to be sung that represents their situation.

SITUATIONS

- A mother and daughter disagree about when the daughter should come home from a party.
- A girl's boyfriend says he wants to marry her, but he doesn't want a temple wedding. He says that he wants her to have a big, fancy wedding where she can feel special. He feels that they can always go to the temple later.
- A family must decide whether to go to church on Sunday or begin their vacation a day early.
- Your little brother wants to play with you and your friend, but he's really a pain and never plays right.
- Two sisters have been fighting. Each is sure that she is right and the other is being mean and unfair.
- Your brother put a dent in dad's car but he isn't going to tell. He says your dad will never notice, or will just think he did it himself.
- You are hungry, but your mother is sick and can't fix you something to eat.

9. The Priesthood Is Restored

Children's Songbook p. 96

Opening Song: **The Fifth Article of Faith** *Children's Songbook* p. 125

Closing Song: **The Priesthood Is Restored** *Children's Songbook* p. 96

Materials Needed

- Copy of the word puzzle on transparency film
- Overhead projector. (If this is not available in your unit, copy the word puzzle onto the chalkboard or a piece of poster board.)
- Dry erase marker
- Use a computer and printer, free hand, or stencils to create alphabet letters that are 6 or 7 inches high
- Tape or other fasteners

Preparation

- Color, if needed, and cut out the alphabet letters.
- Write the activities and questions from below on the backs of letters A, D, E, G, H, I, K, M, N, O, P, R, S, T, U, and W.
- Place all the letters of the alphabet in visible places around room.

Teaching Suggestions

Introduce this song by melody only. Have the children quietly hum along with the piano. Tell them that the words to this new song announce something wonderful that has happened in the past. They must figure out the message by solving a puzzle.

Show the children the word puzzle by using the overhead projector to broadcast it onto a blank surface. You might have them hum along again while you point to the word blanks that would fit each note.

Point out the three places in the song where one note is held for two measures. Challenge them to watch you to see if they can hum, and later sing, that note as long as it is held. When those three words are learned, demonstrate how to say the word: by extending the middle vowel section till the end of the musical note, and then add the ending consonants.

Have children take turns choosing letters from around the room.

If the letter fits into the puzzle it will have a scripture, question, or activity on the back of it that must be completed for the letter to be inserted into the puzzle.

If the letter is not needed in the puzzle, it will be blank.

If a letter is used more than once, insert all of them when the letter is chosen. Set the letters aside after they have been chosen so they don't become mixed with those that are left.

Note: This process will go faster if you have another leader helping you write in the letters as they are picked.

As every couple of words is completed, have the children practice the song again by humming the words that are not complete and singing those that are. When the words are complete, sing the whole song one time through, and then add the accompaniment for the big finish.

Activities and Questions

1. Turn around three times.
2. Read D&C 43:1.
3. What is a prophet?
4. Sing the third verse of **On a Golden Springtime** *Children's Songbook* p. 88.
5. Name one thing the priesthood can be used for.
6. What does "restored" mean?
7. Sing **Latter-day Prophets** *Children's Songbook* p. 134.
8. Name one person you know who holds the priesthood.
9. Who was Joseph Smith?
10. Choose a favorite song to sing.
11. Read Joseph Smith—History 1:68–72.
12. Name one thing you can do to follow God's plan for you.
13. What power does a man need to be able to act for God?
14. How does someone receive the priesthood?
15. What is the Fifth Article of Faith?
16. Shake two people's hands.

___ __________

__ ________,

___ _____ ____

_____ __ ___,

____ ___ ___

______ __ ___

_____. ___ ___'_

__ ____ _____.

The Priesthood
is restored,
the truth made
known to man,
that God has
spoken to the
earth. His pow'r
is here again.

10. A Restoration Timeline

Opening Song: **The Priesthood Is Restored** *Children's Songbook* p. 89

Closing Song: **On a Golden Springtime** *Children's Songbook* p. 88

Materials Needed

- Piece of string or yarn (at least 95 inches long)
- *Gospel Art Pictures* #114, 403, 406, 407, 416, 500, 507, 601, 610, 612, and 618
- Tape or other appropriate fasteners
- Eleven clothes pins with spring mechanism
- Large picture of Joseph Smith (or *Gospel Art Picture* #400)

Preparation

- Be familiar with the basic historical accounts before presenting this lesson.
- Mount the picture of Joseph Smith in the front of the Primary room.
- Secure one end of the yarn just below the picture (tying will work best, if possible) and leave the other end free.

Teaching Suggestions

Have one child be your helper. He or she will hold the free end of the string; it should be stretched out so that it is taut. This helper can be changed periodically during the lesson time.

Help the children understand that after Jesus died, there was an apostasy; meaning, His church and teaching began to be changed by men who didn't hold the priesthood. Christ's church eventually disappeared from the earth entirely.

Remind them that we have Christ's true church on the earth today because it was restored through heavenly messengers. The children will help you assemble a timeline that shows some of the steps of the restoration of the gospel.

Have the piano begin playing the first song. Let the children quietly raise their hands when they think they know what the song is. The first child who appropriately names the song gets to hang the corresponding picture on the timeline, using the clothes pins to secure it to the string. Start at the end of string that is closest to the picture.

Briefly describe the concept that each picture represents, and sing the associated song. Continue until all the pictures have been hung on the timeline.

End with your testimony of the restored gospel.

PICTURES AND SUGGESTED SONGS

- **The first vision**—#403 "The First Vision." In 1820, Joseph Smith was confused about which church he should join; he knelt and prayed in a grove of trees near his home. Heavenly Father and Jesus Christ appeared to him and told him he would help restore Christ's true church to the earth. **The Sacred Grove** *Children's Songbook* p. 87.
- **Joseph receives the golden plates**—#406 "Joseph Receives the Gold Plates." Joseph was allowed to take the brass plates, which Moroni had told him about, to translate them. This was not easy and would take Joseph many years to finish. **The Golden Plates** *Children's Songbook* p. 86.
- **The priesthood is restored**—#407 "John the Baptist Conferring the Aaronic Priesthood." While Joseph translated the plates, he sometimes had questions. Praying about one of these questions lead to a visit from John the Baptist where Joseph and Oliver Cowdery received the Aaronic Priesthood. **The Priesthood Is Restored** *Children's Songbook* p. 89.
- **The ordinance of baptism is revealed**—#601 "Baptism." After he gave them the Priesthood, John the Baptist taught Joseph and Oliver about baptism and they were baptized. **I Like My Birthdays** *Children's Songbook* p. 104.
- **The Book of Mormon is published**—#416 "Translating the Book of Mormon." With help from Heavenly Father, Joseph Smith translated the golden plates. The first copies of the Book of Mormon were published in 1830. **Book of Mormon Stories** *Children's Songbook* p. 118.
- **The first missionaries are sent out**—#612 "Missionaries Teach the Gospel of Jesus Christ." As soon as The Book of Mormon was printed, missionaries began sharing it with everyone they could. We still send missionaries all over the world to help people know about the gospel and how it can make us happy. **I Hope They Call Me on a Mission** *Children's Songbook* p. 169.
- **The church is formally organized**—#610 "Sustaining Our Leaders." In April 1830, The Church of Jesus Christ of Latter-day Saints was officially organized. The roles of its leaders were given in a revelation and those leaders were sustained by the members, just as we do today. **The Church of Jesus Christ** *Children's Songbook* p. 77.
- **The Word of Wisdom is revealed**—#114 "Daniel Refusing the King's Meat." Every thing that we are taught in the church today is the same gospel that was established by Jesus from the beginning of the world. One of those teachings is the Word of Wisdom. Daniel knew that some things were not good for his body, and we do too. **The Word of Wisdom** *Children's Songbook* p. 154.
- **The first temple is dedicated**—#500 "Kirtland Temple." How wonderful it is to have temples! We go there to learn more about Heavenly Father and His plan for us; we make covenants with Him and can seal our families together forever. The first temple was dedicated in 1836; today we have more than 120 temples all over the world. **I Love to See the Temple** *Children's Songbook* p. 95.

- **The Articles of Faith are given**—#618 "The Articles of Faith." Joseph Smith was asked if he could write down a summary of what The Church of Jesus Christ of Latter-day Saints believed and stood for. With the help of Heavenly Father, Joseph created a list of 13 things to help us and the world understand the Lord's church better. **The First Article of Faith** *Children's Songbook* p. 122.
- **Priesthood keys continue**—#506 "Latter-day Prophets." Joseph Smith died in June of 1844, but because of his work, the Church did not die with him. Another worthy priesthood holder was called to be the new prophet and we still have a living prophet today. He holds the priesthood and helps us know what Heavenly Father wants us to do. **Latter-day Prophets** *Children's Songbook* p. 134.

SPECIAL NOTE

This year we celebrate the 200th anniversary of Joseph Smith's birth (December 23, 1805). Consider holding an "In the Days of Joseph Smith" activity day.

- Make cornbread and homemade butter
- Make candles
- Hold stick pulling, log rolling and field plowing events
- Mark copies of the Book of Mormon for use by the missionaries

11. FAITH

Children's Songbook p. 96

Opening Song: **A Child's Prayer** *Children's Songbook* p. 12

Closing Song: **Faith** *Children's Songbook* p. 96

MATERIALS NEEDED

- Copy of the flower pot illustration on cardstock
- Copy of leaf illustrations, on green paper, or color them if desired
- Poster board
- Glue
- Green marker
- Tape

PREPARATION

- Glue the flower pot to the poster board (arrange it so that the board is tall instead of wide).
- Draw a thick green stem coming from the pot to the top of the poster board.
- Cut out and laminate the leaf illustrations for durability.
- Tape the leaves to the chalkboard or other display area in a random order.

TEACHING SUGGESTIONS

Read Alma 32:27–28, 42 aloud with the children. Talk about the way a seed grows and what we need to do to help it. Compare that to learning about Heavenly Father and trusting His plan for us.

Tell the children that they will learn a song about building faith. As they learn, they will help the plant grow. Sing the first line of the song to the children, ask them to find the leaf that would represent that phrase and place it at the base of the plant.

Briefly discuss what the words mean. Have the children then help you sing that line. Continue singing and adding leaves up the stock of the plant, reviewing the song to the point they have learned after every few leaves.

Close with your testimony, your knowledge that God lives and loves you. Emphasize how your testimony has grown as you've grown in the gospel.

SPECIAL NOTES

- Consider presenting the children with a few seeds to take home and plant
- Consider holding a "Faith" activity day
- Make a sun craft
- Bake prayer pretzels
- Decorate heart-shaped cookies
- Have "test your strength" stations and a "to earth and back" obstacle course
- Plant flowers on the church grounds or in close neighbor's yards

FAITH

the Lord will hear my prayers

the sun will rise

a swelling within my heart

if planted it will grow

I can return when my life ends

before my mortal birth

Faith is strengthened

in christ who showed the way

12. I'll Follow Him in Faith

Janice Kapp Perry, *Friend*, January 2003, p. 24

Opening Song: **I Believe in Christ** *Hymns* #134

Closing Song: **I'll Follow Him in Faith** *Friend,* January 2003, p. 24

Materials Needed

- 16 sheets of paper (you will need 32 sheets if you hold two singing times)
- Crayons for use by the children

Preparation

- Label the top of each paper with a suggested stanza from below. If you have more children in each presentation group, have them work together or provide extra sheets with the words. If you have fewer children, eliminate duplicates, or phrases may be combined.
- Invite an older class or someone from your ward or branch, to practice this song to sing for the Primary by way of introduction.

Teaching Suggestions

Introduce the person or group that has prepared this song. Emphasize that the singers will be sharing a special message for the children to learn.

When the song is complete, bear your testimony of Jesus Christ and His love for you. Point out the feelings of the Spirit that are present.

Tell the children that you would like them to have a chance to learn about the things they heard in this song. To help them learn the words and think about how much Heavenly Father loves them, they will help you put together visual aids for the song.

Show them the blank papers with the words to the song on them. Have them repeat each one after you read it to them. You might choose to mention some specific ideas that would portray a few of the passages, to help them focus their ideas. Then, pass out the papers to the children and let each of them draw a picture that they think shows the meaning of their assigned words.

Try to save at least 10 minutes at the end to allow the children to come up in groups that follow the verses. Repeat the words with the children and let them show their pictures. Try singing each verse with the children's picture prompts and the piano.

Be sure to store the junior and senior Primary pictures separately for future use in review of this song.

PHRASES FOR THE PAPERS

- The Lord has blessed me with gospel truth.
- I have learned His ways in my early youth.
- I will share my light for I know it's right to testify of Him.
- The Lord has blessed me with simple faith.
- If I pray for help, He will give me strength.
- I will do His work. I will gladly serve.
- I'll follow Him in faith. (2)
- The Lord has blessed me to feel His love.
- I have felt His promptings and learned to trust.
- So in all I do, I'll be faithful to the things I know are true.
- The Lord has blessed me in many ways.
- With a thankful heart I will sing His praise.
- I will raise my voice and proclaim my choice
- To follow Him in faith.
- He has shown the way, and through all my days,

13. Jesus Is My Example

Opening Song: **Tell Me the Stories of Jesus** *Children's Songbook* p. 57

Closing Song: **I'm Trying to Be like Jesus** *Children's Songbook* p. 78

Materials Needed

- 8 Copies of the footprint illustration
- Chalkboard or other display area
- Tape or other appropriate fasteners
- Favorite picture of Christ
- 2 Magnets, or other method to use as playing pieces
- Numbered spinner, taken from a family board game, with no more than 5 or 6 numbers on the face
- 20 index cards
- Set of Scriptures for use by the children

Preparation

- Cut the feet apart, color if desired.
- Write "Sing!" on 10 of the feet.
- Write a question mark on 10 of the feet.
- Mount the picture of Christ at the top right hand side of the chalkboard.
- Place the feet randomly on a path across the chalkboard, leading to the picture of Christ.
- Write one of the situations/scriptures from below on the index cards. Label them on the reverse side with a question mark. Mix them up. Place them face down in a pile.

Teaching Suggestions

Tell the children that they will be playing a game to help them remember some of the things they can do to be more like Jesus. Divide them into two teams.

Children will take turns spinning the spinner and moving through the footstep game spaces.

If a child lands on a song footprint, they must choose their favorite song about Jesus for all the children to sing.

If they land on a question mark, they are to draw an index card. Their group must then look up and read the scripture, or give a Christlike solution to the problem on the question card.

Continue the game until both teams have made it to the picture of Jesus.

SITUATIONS AND SCRIPTURES

- Your mother wants you to go with her to stay with an elderly neighbor, but you don't like the way his house smells, and he can't talk right.
- A boy at school begins yelling at you and calling you names. He says you stole something from him but you didn't.
- Some friends of yours want you to come home with them after school, but when they asked you got a sick feeling in your stomach.
- You've been thinking that you should say "hi" to the new girl all day.
- You came home from school and found that your little sister broke all your crayons.
- You are playing kickball with your friends, but some of the other team members are being mean and cheating.
- Your friends keep talking during the lesson at church, you think you might as well join in because the lesson is one you have already heard a million times and you're bored.
- You can't see why your Primary leaders say you should memorize the *Articles of Faith.*
- You have a friend who did something very wrong. He says he isn't going to go talk to the Bishop about it until he's older, because there is plenty of time to repent later.
- Your friend says he doesn't want to be baptized. He says it seems silly to him, and he's not sure if the church is true.
- Matthew 4:23
- Matthew 5:44
- John 13:14–15
- 2 Nephi 9:23
- 2 Nephi 25:26
- 3 Nephi 17:21–23
- 3 Nephi 27:21
- Moroni 7:48
- D&C 19:23
- Articles of Faith 1:4

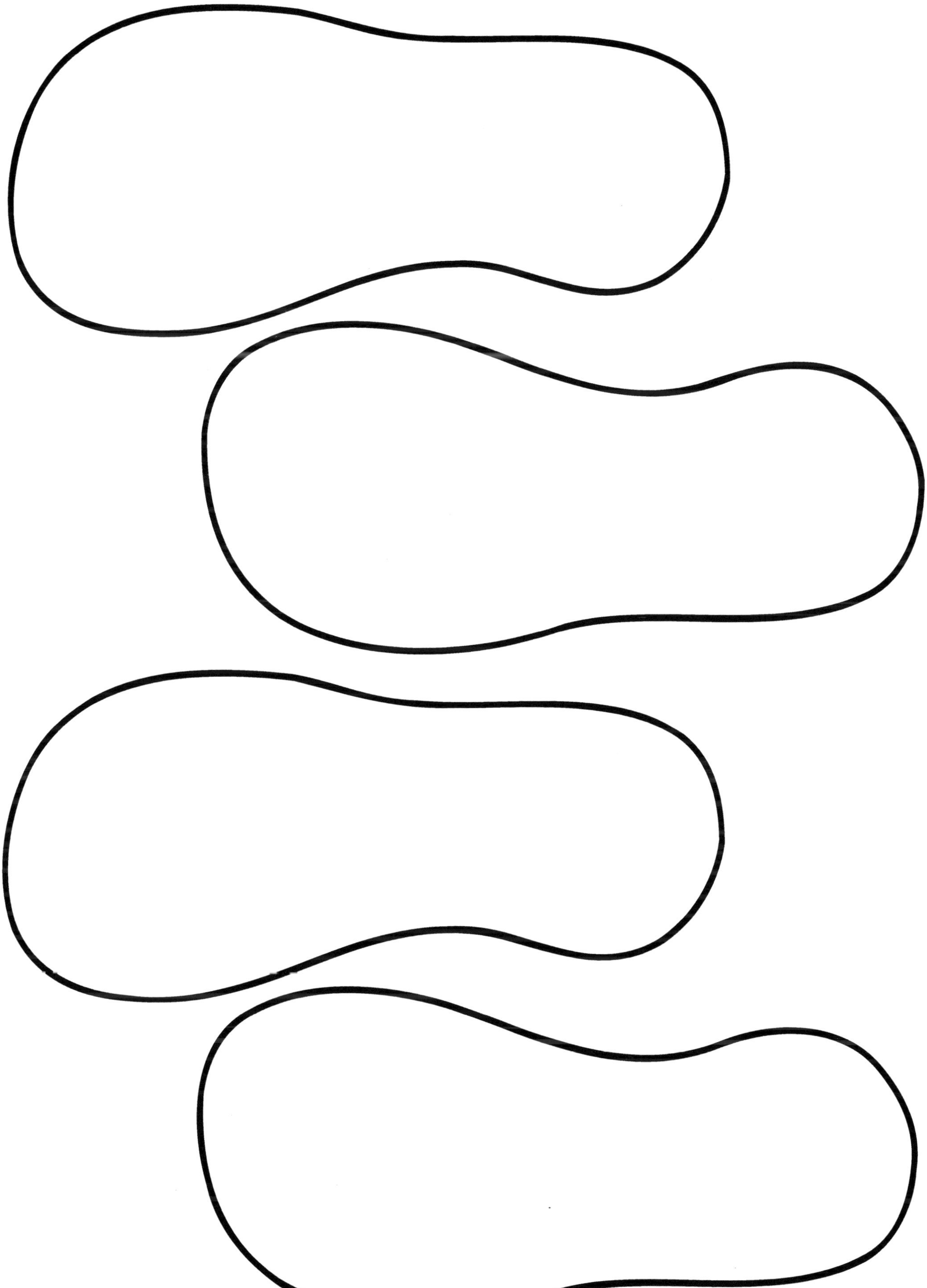

14. When I Am Baptized

Children's Songbook p. 103

Opening Song: **I Will Follow God's Plan** *Children's Songbook* p. 164

Closing Song: **When I am Baptized** *Children's Songbook* p. 103

Materials Needed

- Copies of the illustrations on cardstock quality paper
- 5 Pieces of brown construction paper
- 6 Large craft sticks
- Scissors
- Glue
- *Gospel Art Picture* #103
- Tape
- Chalkboard or other display area
- Book of Mormon
- Bar of soap and wash cloth

Preparation

- Be familiar with the story of Noah, the ark, and the promise of the rainbow from the back of the *Gospel Art Picture.*
- Color all the illustrations.
- Cut out the small images, and glue them to the craft sticks, leaving enough stick exposed to use as a handle.
- Cut the large rainbow into its separate strips.
- Cut the brown construction paper into 5 large, free-form puddles or dirt images.

Teaching Suggestions

Introduce today's lesson by stating the song's title and asking the children what they think the song will talk about. Allow them to share their thoughts on baptism with you.

Share 2 Nephi 9:23 with the children. Impress upon the children that there are 6 main reasons why Heavenly Father wants us to be baptized. Display each strip of the large rainbow, starting with "To follow Jesus' example" and work your way up. Briefly explain each statement as it is placed.

Ask the children to tell you what you have made on the board (a rainbow). Introduce the first line of the song at this time. Show the rainbow stick symbol, say the phrase and have the children repeat it back to you.

Next, show the picture of Noah. Briefly tell the story of the ark, the cleansing of the earth and the promise of the rainbow. Be sure to emphasize how thankful Noah was to see the rainbow and to know that the world was clean and pure again.

Show the earth and share the next line of the song. Have the children repeat it back to you. Then, put the first two lines together and repeat them with the children. Listen to the piano play the verse for them to hear, and then try singing along one time.

Have a leader come up to help you with the next explanation (do not choose a child, as you do not want them to internalize or feel criticized by the demonstration). Explain to the children that just as Heavenly Father needed to cleanse the earth of sin and the things that were going wrong, we need that same chance. We were given agency when we came to earth, and Heavenly Father knew we would not always do what was right.

When we do something wrong, it's like adding dirt to our spirits; just like playing in the mud would get our bodies dirty. Place the paper mud spots all over the leader that is helping you. With each spot you place, state an imagined wrong choice that they could have made (i.e., yelled at their sister this morning, forgot to read their scriptures all week, cheated on a test, etc.).

Ask the children how she can become clean again. Show the soap and wash cloth. Just like we need to wash our bodies when we get dirty, baptism washes our spirits clean. Because of the atonement of Jesus Christ, everyone can be clean again and return to Heavenly Father.

After we are baptized, we will still make mistakes; but, we are given the sacrament to help us remember our baptism and the atonement, and help us do what is right. When we do make a mistake, repentance will wipe away the dirt again.

Briefly explain the process of repentance.

At this time, share the stick images of baptism and improving steps. Repeat the words, listen to the piano and have the children try to sing the second verse.

Challenge the children to strive for clean lives and a desire to be with Heavenly Father again. Then, introduce the chorus illustrations of the soap and the ribbon. Tell the children that the chorus is a statement of a child's conviction to keep his baptismal covenants.

Go back to the first verse and choose reverent children to come up and hold the stick prompts while you sing the entire first verse and chorus. Then, choose new children to hold the prompts for the second verse and chorus.

End with your testimony of gratitude for baptism, the atonement and sacrament, and the chance to continually repent and try to be better so you can live with Heavenly Father again.

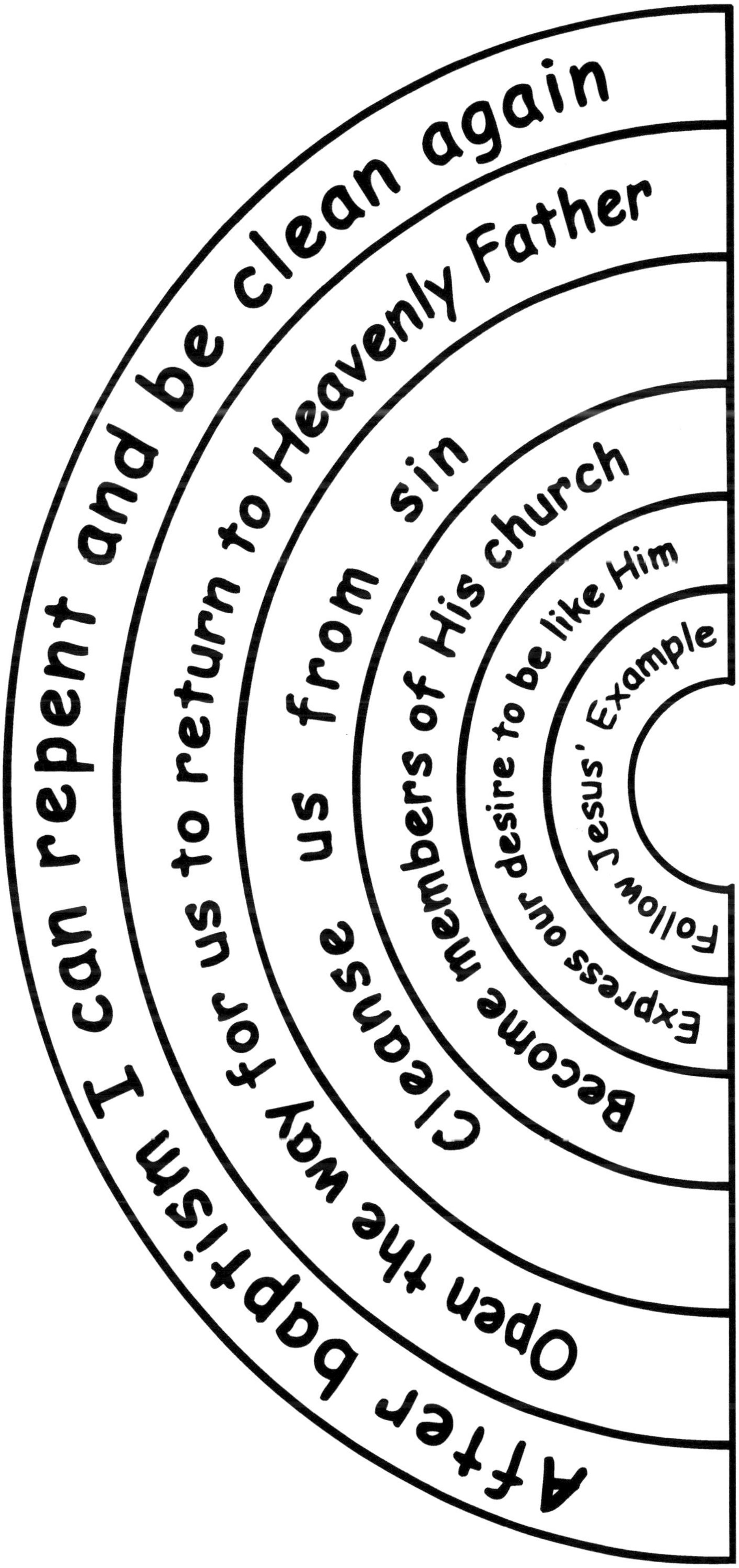
After baptism I can repent and be clean again
Open the way for us to return to Heavenly Father
Cleanse us from sin
Become members of His church
Express our desire to be like Him
Follow Jesus' Example

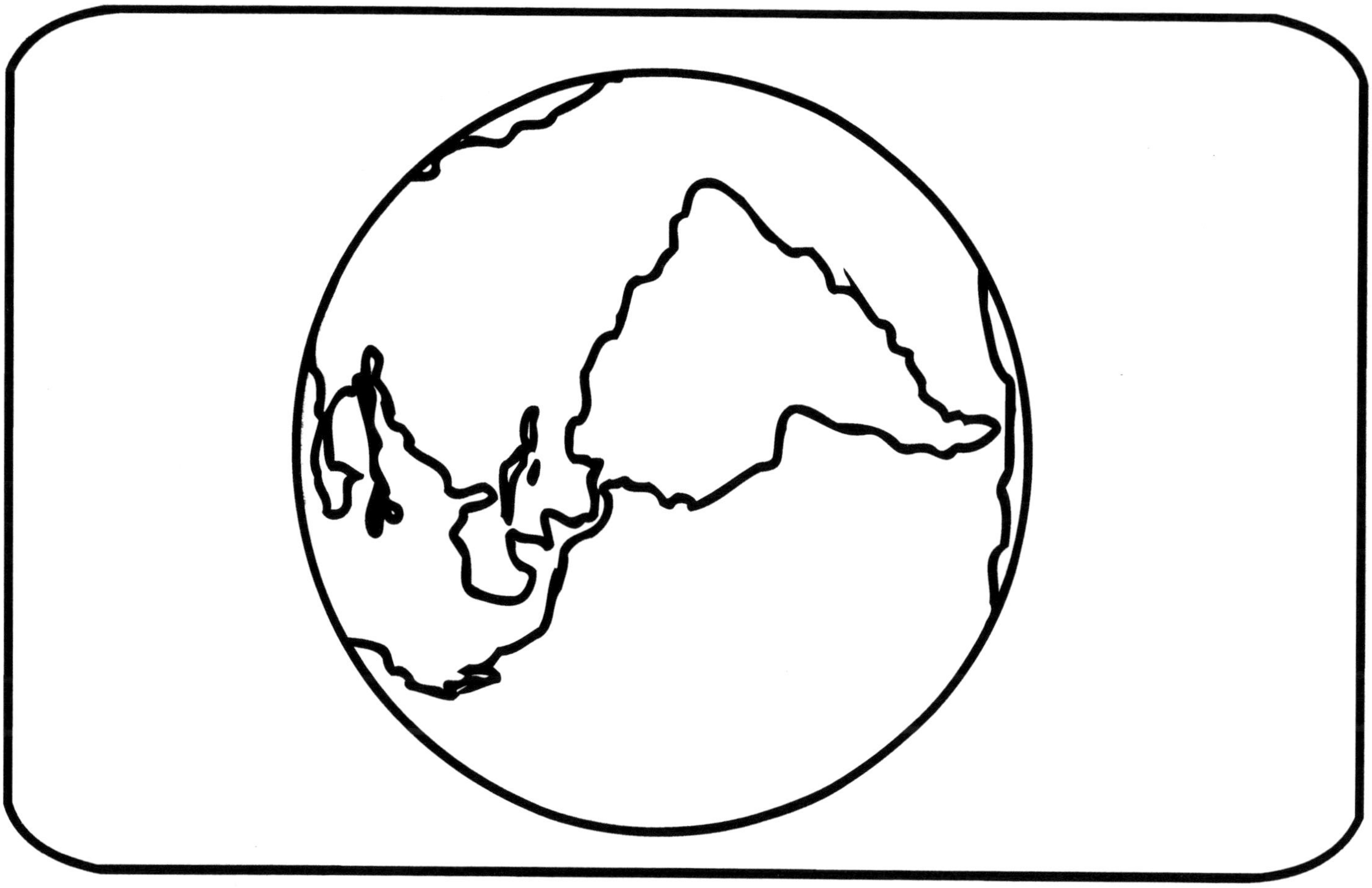

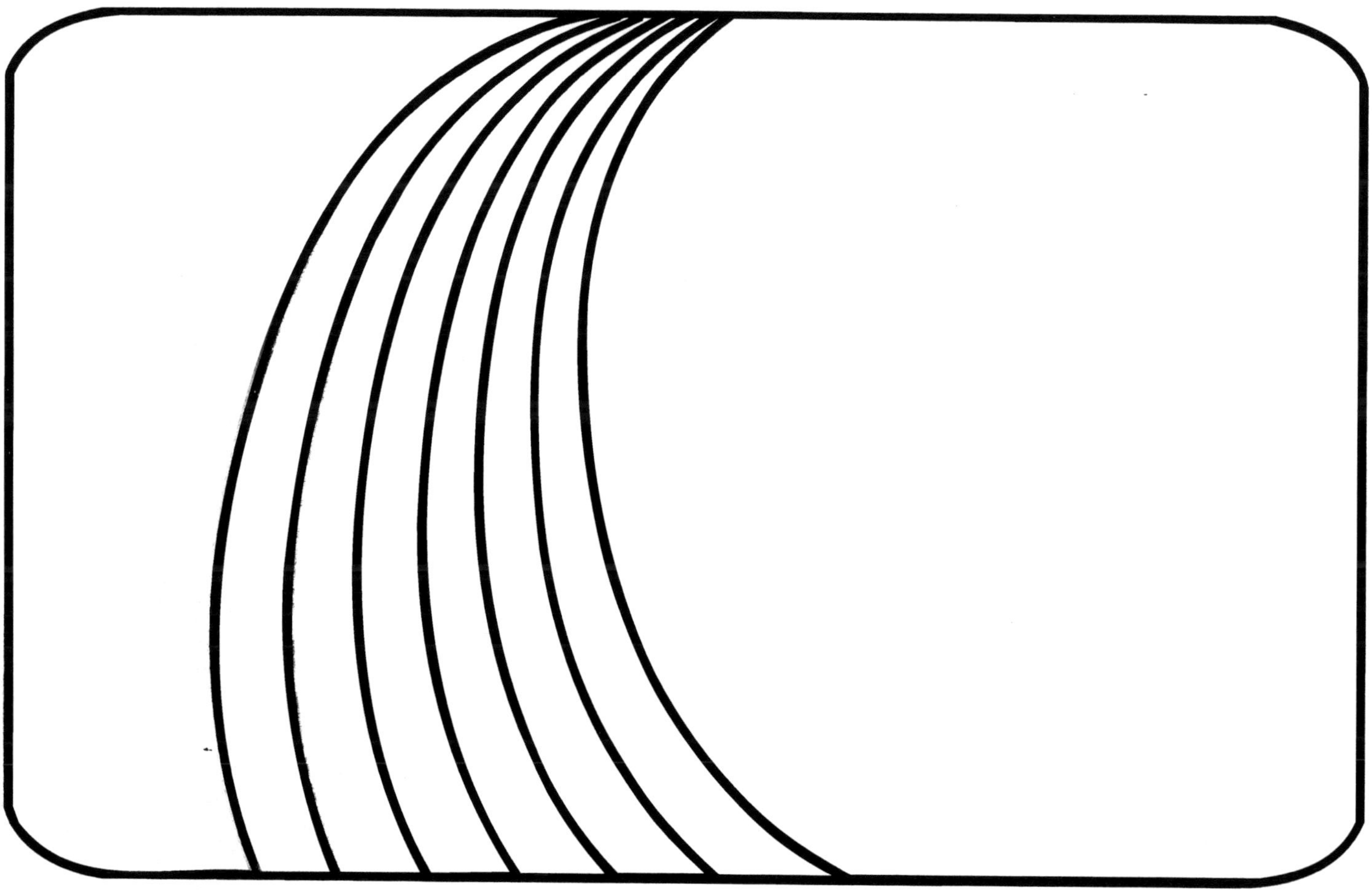

IMPROVE

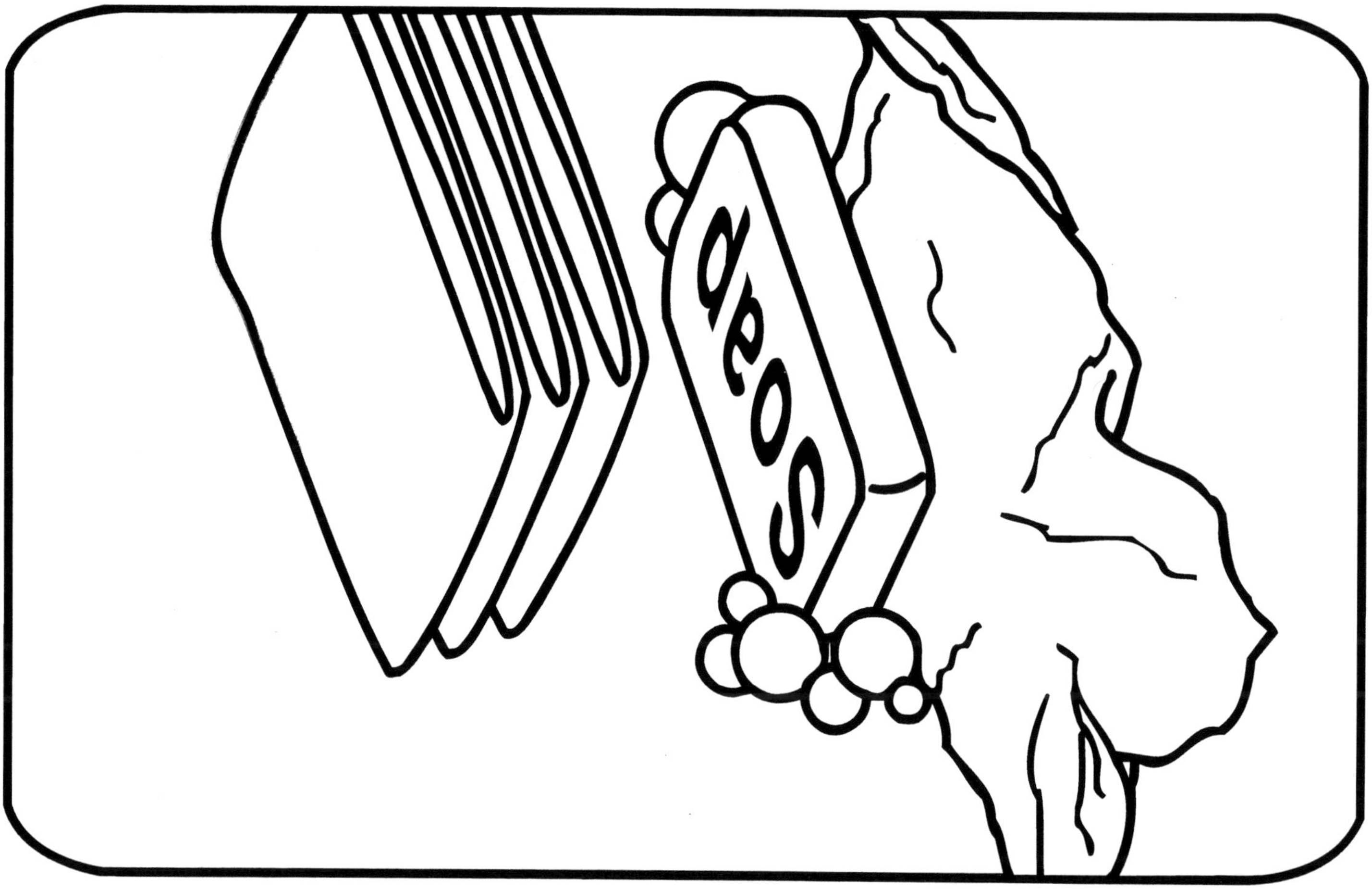
Soap

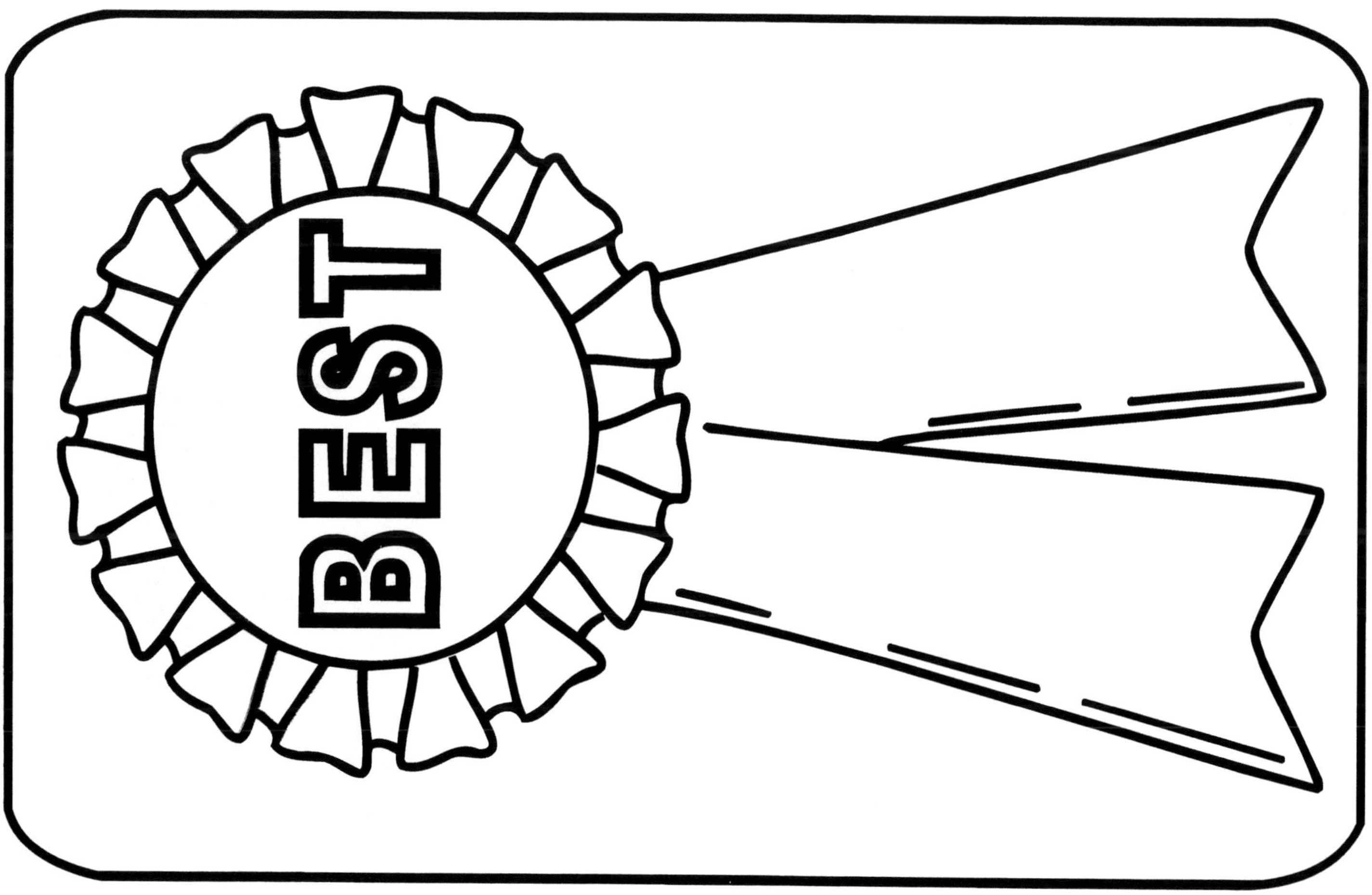
BEST

15. My Baptismal Covenants

Opening Song: **I Will Follow God's Plan** *Children's Songbook* p. 164

Closing Song: **When I am Baptized** *Children's Songbook* p. 103

Materials Needed

- Copy of illustrations, enlarged to 11x17
- Tape
- Scriptures for use by children

Preparation

- Color the illustrations.
- Laminate the reverent baptism picture for durability.
- Cut out the silly mistake images. These may be laminated as well or left as is.
- Write a number for each song or scripture on the back of each mistake image.
- Tape the silly images over the reverent scene. Refer to the smaller inset illustration as a guide for proper placement.
- Invite the full-time missionaries to share a brief message about the importance of baptism and what happens when someone is baptized.

Teaching Suggestions

Introduce the missionaries and allow them to share their message with the children.

Show the children your prepared illustration. Tell them that the picture is supposed to show a baptism.

Ask them if they think this picture is correct.

Remind the children what they have learned: baptism washes away all of their mistakes, it makes them clean again. The children will help you fix the picture as they review more about baptism and the covenants that we make when we are baptized. This is like being baptized, or repenting. When they are finished the picture will look more like what Heavenly Father wants it to.

Choose reverent children to come up and identify things that are wrong or out of place. Remove that item and read and discuss the scripture or sing the song listed on the back.

After all the pieces have been removed, end with your testimony of your own baptism and the importance of taking the sacrament to remember the covenants we have made.

SCRIPTURES AND SONGS

- **When Jesus Christ Was Baptized** *Children's Songbook* p. 102
- **I'll Follow Him in Faith** Janice Kapp Perry *Friend*, January 2003, p. 24
- **The Sacrament** *Children's Songbook* p. 72
- **I Believe in Christ** *Hymns* #134
- Acts 2:38
- Mosiah 18:8–10
- 3 Nephi 18:7
- 3 Nephi 18:11
- D&C 68:27
- Articles of Faith 1:4

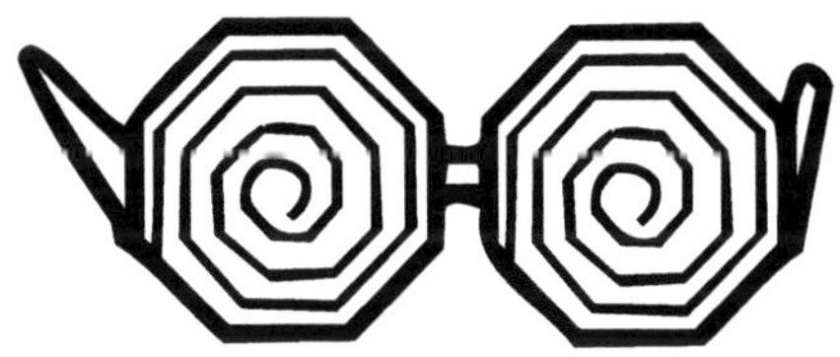

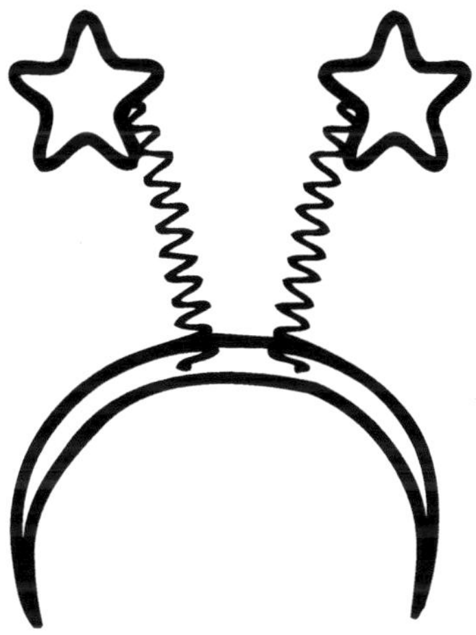

16. The Holy Ghost

Children's Songbook p. 105

Opening Song: **I Know My Father Lives** *Children's Songbook* p. 5

Closing Song: **The Holy Ghost** *Children's Songbook* p. 105

Materials Needed

- Chalk and chalkboard
- Holy Bible
- *Gospel Art Picture* #216 "Christ and the Children"

Preparation

- Prayerfully review John 14:26–27 and be familiar with the entry of "Holy Ghost" in the *Bible Dictionary.*

Teaching Suggestions

Ask the children if someone they love has ever gone away for a long time (perhaps a sibling or grandparents on a mission). How did they stay in touch? How did the child know that the person still loved and cared for them? Allow them to briefly share their experiences.

Show the picture of Christ. Explain that while Jesus was on the earth, many people loved Him and liked to be near Him. Jesus knew that He would have to leave all these people behind and they would be sad. Some might even think He didn't love them any more. What could Jesus do to help them remember Him and know that He loved them? Allow the children to share their thoughts with you.

Read John 14:26–27 to the children. Ask them to tell you what these verses talk about (the Holy Ghost).

Ask the children what the Holy Ghost can do for us. List their answers on the chalkboard.

The Holy Ghost is sometimes called the "still small voice." If we want to hear and feel all the things the Holy Ghost would like to tell us, we must learn to be quiet and listen.

Have the children try this activity. Instruct them be as quiet as they can for between 30 seconds and one minute so they can listen to things around them. Afterward, let them share some of the things they were able to hear. You might choose to write these on the chalkboard.

Next introduce the song by telling the children they will be playing an echo game to learn about the Holy Ghost. They must be as quiet as they can and listen while you whisper each line, and then see if they can repeat it back to you. After they say each set of words correctly introduce the melody and sing that line.

Go through all the words, and then choose children to help you prompt each verse. Each child will be assigned a line from the verse to repeat. After each child says his line, the rest of the children respond by singing it back to him. Repeat the procedure for the second verse, and then put the entire song together without interruptions.

Commend the children for their efforts in listening. Encourage them to try and find quiet times to feel the Holy Ghost in their own lives. Testify of His power to influence and direct their lives and help them feel the Savior's love.

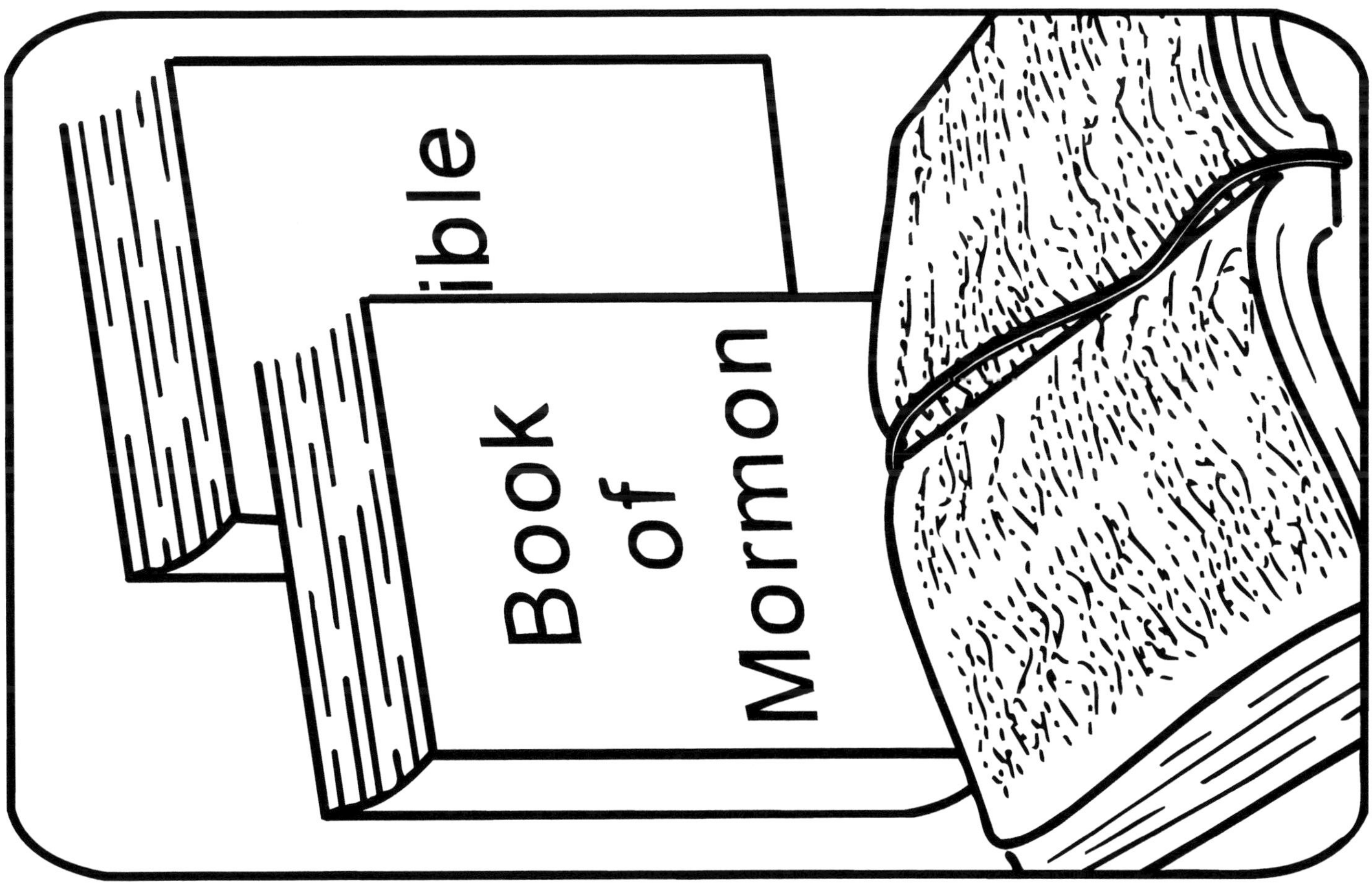
ible
Book
of
Mormon

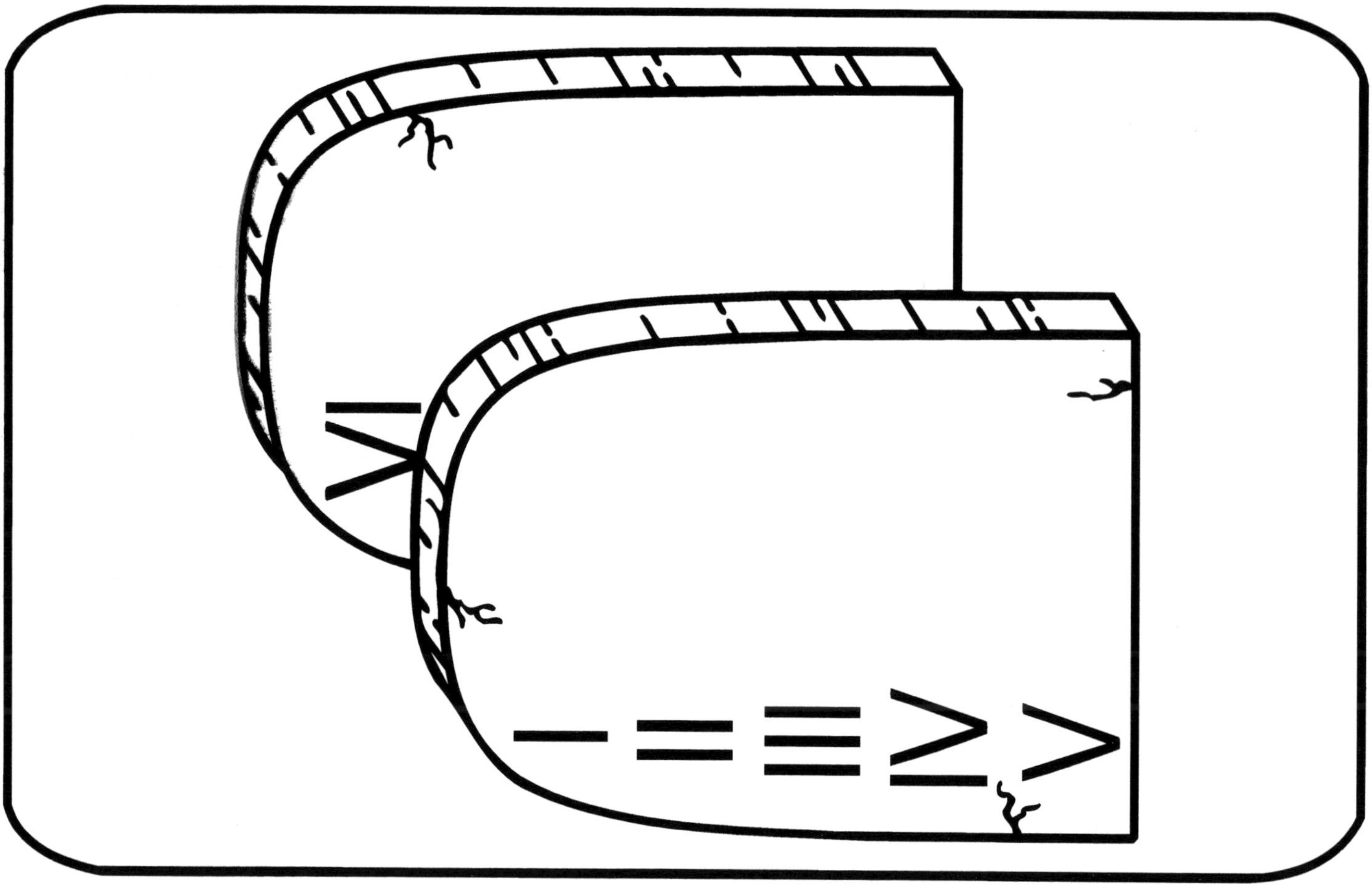
I
II
III
IV
V
VI

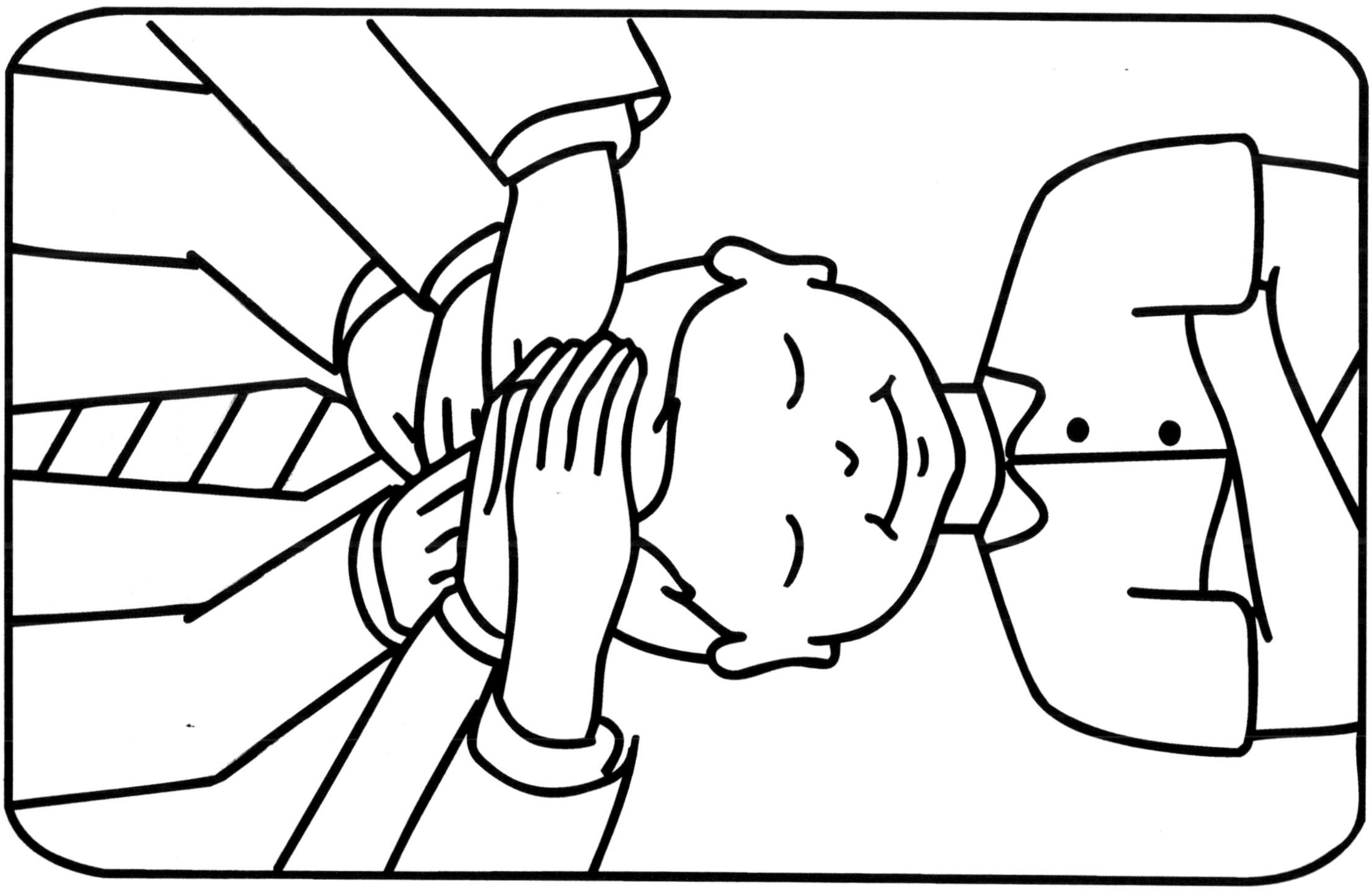

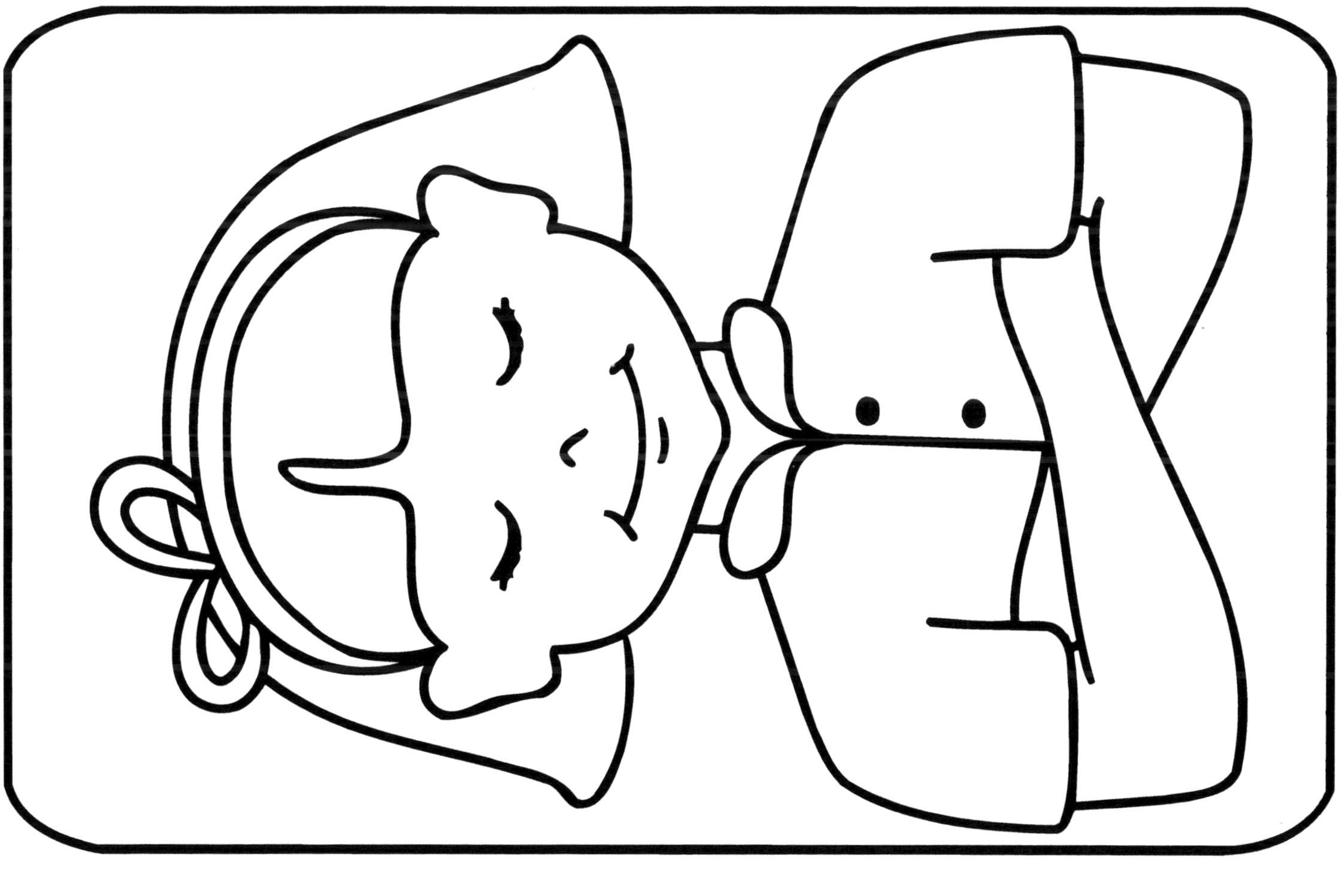

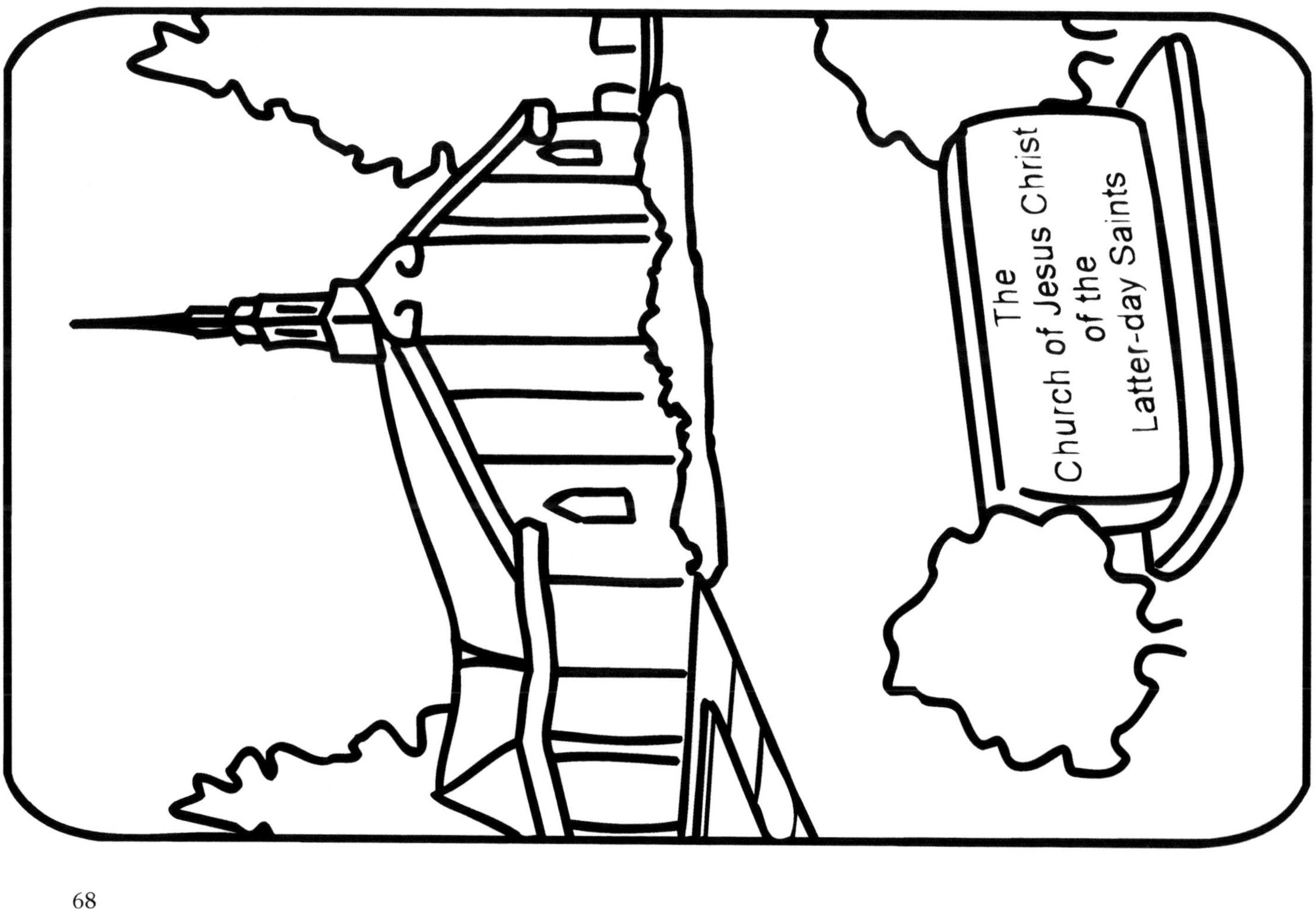
The
Church of Jesus Christ
of the
Latter-day Saints

17. THE GIFT OF THE HOLY GHOST

Opening Song: **The Holy Ghost** *Children's Songbook* p. 105

Closing Song: **The Still Small Voice** *Children's Songbook* p. 106

MATERIALS NEEDED

- A large comforter or quilt
- Rocking chair or other comfortable chair
- Copy of included illustrations
- *Gospel Art Picture* #107 "Moses and the Burning Bush"
- Tape
- Scriptures
- Chalk and chalkboard

PREPARATION

- Be familiar with the story of Moses found in Exodus 3:1–5.
- Color and cut out the illustrations, write the corresponding song number on the backs.

TEACHING SUGGESTIONS

Start by asking the children to describe everything that they know about the Holy Ghost and His purpose in each of our lives. You might choose to write some of their ideas on the chalkboard.

Ask one of the children to sit down in the rocking chair, wrap up in your quilt, and rock quietly for a minute. Ask all of the children to think of a time when they have been scared, nervous, or alone, and to remember what those feelings were like.

Have the child in the quilt try and share what it feels like to be safe and comfortable. Remind the children to think of how it felt when their feelings of anxiety were relieved; also, have them think of times when they have felt happy and at peace. Have a few of them try to share how they felt at those times.

Help the children realize that feelings of comfort and peace are from the Holy Ghost.

Read John 14:16–17 with the children.

Feelings are not always easy to understand or recognize. Understanding how the Holy Ghost works will help us to identify what it feels like when the Spirit is with us. As we become more aware of these feelings, we will feel the presence of the Spirit with us more often.

The Holy Ghost is there to lead, teach, and comfort us, and to show us how to become more like Jesus Christ. It is through His influence that we gain our testimonies of Jesus Christ.

When we are baptized and confirmed a member of The Church of Jesus Christ of Latter-day Saints, we are given the gift of the Holy Ghost. If we live worthily, He will be our companion. We can feel the influence of the Holy Ghost even before we are baptized, but He can't stay with us until after we have been given that gift by a worthy priesthood holder.

Show the children the picture of Moses and share the story depicted. Help them realize that Moses had to prepare himself to hear the message of the Lord by removing something of himself that represented the world: that was his shoes. The more we practice removing worldly things from our lives and begin looking towards those things that we have been asked to do, the more we will be able to have the Spirit as our companion.

Show the children the pictures you posted of ways they can remove the world and draw closer to the Holy Ghost so He can dwell with us. Have reverent children come up and choose a picture, tell what it would symbolize and then sing the song off the back of the picture.

PICTURE AND CORRESPONDING SONGS

- Baptism (be baptized) **When I Am Baptized** *Children's Songbook* p. 103
- Confirmation (receive the gift of the Holy Ghost) **The Holy Ghost** *Children's Songbook* p. 105
- Scriptures (scripture study) **Search, Ponder and Pray** *Children's Songbook* p. 146
- Child Praying (prayer) **A Child's Prayer** *Children's Songbook* p. 12
- Church Building (attending our meetings) **The Chapel Doors** *Children's Songbook* p. 156
- Bread and Fruit (living the Word of Wisdom) **The Word of Wisdom** *Children's Songbook* p. 154
- Media devices (keeping what we read, watch and listen to appropriate) **Hum Your Favorite Hymn** *Children's Songbook* p. 152
- Ten Commandments (keeping the commandments) **Keep the Commandments** *Children's Songbook* p. 146

18. CHOOSE THE RIGHT WAY

Children's Songbook p. 160

Opening Song: **I Will Follow God's Plan** *Children's Songbook* p. 164

Closing Song: **Choose the Right Way** *Children's Songbook* p. 160

MATERIALS NEEDED

- Construction paper
- Scissors
- 10 index cards
- Holy Bible

PREPARATION

- Write the song, in musical phrases, on strips of construction paper.
- Write the scenarios on the index cards.
- Hide the word strips around the room, noting on the index cards the correct location for the right answer. Then, create a false location for the wrong answer and write it on the card as well. Number the index cards so that word strips will be hunted for in order of the song.

TEACHING SUGGESTIONS

Ask the children to review with you some of the things Heavenly Father has asked us to do. Why does He want us to do these things? Heavenly Father gave us a plan to follow that would help us to be happy while we are here on this earth. He gave us agency to choose for ourselves and promises to bless us when our choices are right.

Read John 13:17 with the children. Assure them that they have been taught the things they need to do to be happy. Relate your testimony of the truthfulness of the gospel. It helps us to be happy and return to Heavenly Father again. Challenge the children to remember to try to choose the right in everything that they do.

Tell the children that they will be going on a treasure hunt for the words to the new song. There will be a problem on the index card to read. When they decide on the right answer to the problem, they will be lead to a piece of the puzzle. As each set of words is found, review them and then try singing that portion with the piano. Occasionally, start at the beginning and sing as far as you have learned.

Remember to congratulate the children for their ability to make right choices and challenge them to try harder during the coming week to choose the right way in everything they do. Bear your testimony of the happiness that trying to do what is right can bring.

SCENARIOS

- **You can see your neighbor's test paper.** If you should check your answers, look___________ If you should do your own work, look___________
- **Your mother told you not to watch TV while she's gone.** If you sneak and watch any way, look___________ If you obey, look___________
- **Your brother just hit you on the arm.** If you should walk away, look___________ If you hit him back, look___________
- **You're tired and don't want to say your prayers.** If you say them anyway, look___________ If you go to bed without saying them, look___________
- **Your friends are throwing rocks at the street sign.** If you throw rocks too, look___________ If you ask them if they will play ball instead, look___________
- **An older boy offers you a cigarette.** If you say no, look___________ If you try it, look___________
- **Your mom asks you to take out the trash.** If you do it, look___________ If you grumble and say you'll do it later, look___________
- **You'd rather talk to your friend than listen to your Primary lesson.** If you talk to your friend, look___________ If you listen respectfully, look___________
- **Your mom says you may have one cookie for a snack.** If you only eat one, look___________ If you sneak an extra when she's not looking, look___________
- **There is a new girl in your class.** If you try to be friendly, look___________ If you ignore her, look___________

19. The Ten Commandments

Opening Song: **Choose the Right Way** *Children's Songbook* p. 160

Closing Song: **Keep the Commandments** *Children's Songbook* p. 146

Materials Needed

- Copy of the commandment tablets from **The Gift of the Holy Ghost** lesson
- Several copies of the Bible for use by children
- Copy of situations for discussion
- Chalkboard
- Chalk

Preparation

- Color, cut and laminate the illustration for durability.

Teaching Suggestions

Help the children locate the Ten Commandments as written in Exodus 20:1–17. As you read through these verses with the children, identify each commandment. Write them in order on the board.

Help them clarify and understand the meanings of each of the commandments by sharing the scenarios from below for them to quickly problem solve with, and discuss how the commandments affect their lives each day.

After each commandment has been discussed, choose two reverent children to assist with the song. One child will leave the room while the other child hides the commandment illustration somewhere in the room. The child who left is then invited back in to look for the hidden commandments, while the rest of the children sing the song. They will help him look by singing louder the closer he comes to the picture, and softer when he is far away.

Commandment Scenarios

- **Commandment #1**—When Matthew's older brother came home from college, he said he didn't believe the Church was true any more. He thought that it was much more important to be able to learn and study, and think for himself. He said he was tired of something he couldn't see or prove telling him what he could or couldn't do. He said knowledge was the only God he believed in.

- **Commandment #2**—Sarah just adores a certain movie star. She has his poster all over her room and spends all her money on his movies. She reads all the gossip papers and books about him. Sometimes she gets in trouble at school for daydreaming about him. On Sunday, the Primary had a lesson about the Israelites worshiping a golden calf. Their teacher warned them not to put other things before God, or to pretend that something is a God that isn't, but that's not the same thing as liking a movie star, is it?
- **Commandment #3**—Jamie's favorite song on the radio uses one of Heavenly Father's names in it several times, but it's not really a reverent song. She wonders if it's still OK as long as she just ignores those parts and doesn't sing those words when she listens.
- **Commandment #4**—Samantha's cousin is visiting for the weekend. She asks if Samantha will take her to the shopping mall on Sunday.
- **Commandment #5**—James hates it when his mother tells him to clean his room. What difference does it make if his room is messy?
- **Commandment #6**—Henry and Josh want to see if they can hit a squirrel with their paintball guns, just to practice. Seth is worried that they might hurt the squirrel. He's also worried that his friends will think he's silly for caring.
- **Commandment #7**—Terry has an older sister who brags about how many boys she's kissed. She says she doesn't want to ever get married and be stuck with just one person forever.
- **Commandment #8**—Last week Justin saw a boy steal a pack of baseball cards from the store. He never got caught and he got away with some really cool cards. Now, Justin thinks it would be okay to take a candy bar since he forgot his lunch.
- **Commandment #9**—Emily told Julia a secret about their friend Robin. Julia wasn't sure if the secret was true or not, but she was pretty sure Robin wouldn't want everyone to know about it. Then, she heard someone else talking about Robin and her secret. Would it be all right if she talked to them about it, since they seemed to already know?
- **Commandment #10**—Colby's best friend just got a new bike. It's the same bike that Colby had asked for on his last birthday. He hadn't gotten it because his dad said it was too expensive. Colby doesn't think his friend deserves to have such a nice bike when he couldn't have one himself. Colby decided he just wouldn't be his friend anymore.

20. The Lord Gave Me a Temple

Children's Songbook p. 153

Opening Song: **I Will Follow God's Plan** *Children's Songbook* p. 164

Closing Song: **The Lord Gave Me a Temple** *Children's Songbook* p. 153

Materials Needed

- Large hand mirror
- *Gospel Art Picture* #403 "The First Vision"
- *Gospel Art Picture* #505 "Washington Temple"
- Tape
- Holy Bible
- Chalk and chalkboard

Preparation

- Write the words to this song on the chalkboard. Replace a few of the words with simplistic drawings (i.e., line-drawing temples and house, stick figure body, stick figure made with dotted lines for spirit, etc.)

Teaching Suggestions

Show the children the mirror you brought. Take the mirror around the room, giving the children a chance to look at their reflection. Ask several children to name something that they liked about what they saw. Provide some other ideas to reinforce theirs.

Remind the children that our bodies, and our lives, are gifts from Heavenly Father. We are his children and we were created in His image. Show the children the picture of the first vision to reinforce that Heavenly Father has a body just like theirs.

Read 1 Corinthians 3:16 with the children. Ask them what this verse says we are (temples). Show the picture of the Washington Temple. Ask the children to share some of the things that make temples special. These ideas can and should include things visible and things that the temple is used for.

Our bodies are just as special and important. Heavenly Father expects us to treat our bodies with respect and to take care of them. Ask the children to share some ideas on how they can take care of and respect their bodies that Heavenly Father gave them.

The song they will learn today shares this same special message. Show the words and talk with the children about what each phrase means as it is covered. Practice singing the phrases individually. When the whole song has been talked about, try singing it one time through without stopping.

Next, ask the children questions pertaining to the message and words of the song such as: "What were we when we lived in heaven?" "How do we keep our spirits free?" "What happens on resurrection morning?" Children who can give correct answers are allowed to come up and erase words from the song, until only your sketches are left. The images should not be erased; they will serve as a silent reminder of the basic concept of the song. Repeat the words and sing the song through frequently.

The message of this song is very important for the children to understand. Remember to bear strong testimony to the children of the beauty of their bodies and the importance of keeping our personal temples clean and pure in every way.

21. My Gospel Standards

Opening Song: **Teach Me to Walk in the Light** *Children's Songbook* p. 177

Closing Song: **The Church of Jesus Christ** *Children's Songbook* p. 77

Materials Needed

- Poster of My Gospel Standards
- Copy of smiley faces
- Tape

Preparation

- Color and cut out the smiley faces.
- Number the backs of the faces 1 through 12.

Teaching Suggestions

Show the children the poster of standards. Explain that this is a way for us to know how to make good choices and be able to do the things that will keep us close to our Heavenly Father. When we are doing these things we are happy and blessed. We are also a blessing to those around us.

Read over the standards with them, and then allow the children to pick a smiley face. Each one will point to a different part of the poster for the children to discuss with you. Ask them a question about what they think the passage means, or ask them to give you an example of how it might be applied to their lives.

After the passage has been briefly discussed, have the children sing the corresponding song.

Phrases and Songs

1. "I will follow Heavenly Father's plan for me." **I Will Follow God's Plan** *Children's Songbook* p. 164.
2. "I will remember the baptismal covenant and listen to the Holy Ghost." **The Holy Ghost** *Children's Songbook* p. 105.
3. "I will choose the right. I know I can repent when I make a mistake." **Choose the Right Way** *Children's Songbook* p. 160.

4. "I will be honest with Heavenly Father, others, and myself." **I Believe in Being Honest** *Children's Songbook* p. 149.
5. "I will use the names of Heavenly Father and Jesus Christ reverently. I will not swear or use crude words." **Hum Your Favorite Hymn** *Children's Songbook* p. 152.
6. "I will do those things on the Sabbath that will help me feel close to Heavenly Father and Jesus Christ." **Remember the Sabbath Day** *Children's Songbook* p. 155.
7. "I will honor my parents and do my part to strengthen my family." **Love is Spoken Here** *Children's Songbook* p. 190.
8. "I will keep my mind and body sacred and pure, and I will not partake of things that are harmful to me." **The Lord Gave Me a Temple** *Children's Songbook*, p. 153.
9. "I will dress modestly to show respect for Heavenly Father and myself." **I am a Child of God** *Children's Songbook* p. 2.
10. "I will only read and watch things that are pleasing to Heavenly Father. I will only listen to music that is pleasing to Heavenly Father." **The Thirteenth Article of Faith** *Children's Songbook* p. 132.
11. "I will seek good friends and treat others kindly." **Friends are Fun** *Children's Songbook* p. 262.
12. "I will live now to be worthy to go to the temple, serve a mission, and do my part to have an eternal family." **I Love to See the Temple** *Children's Songbook* p. 95.

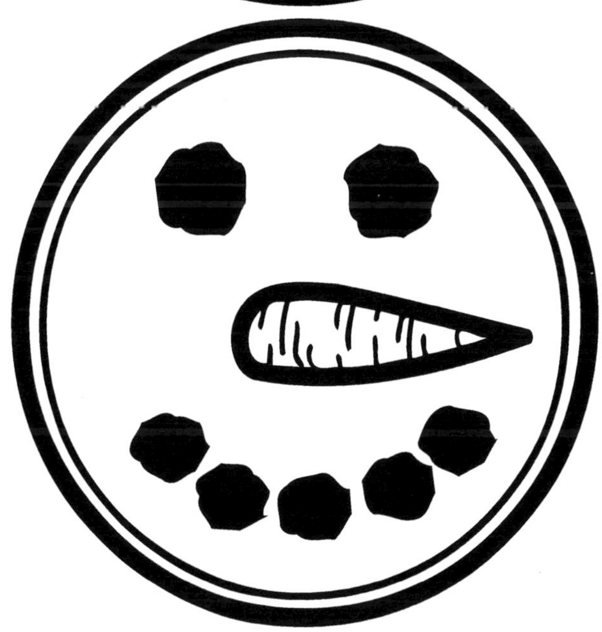

22. I Will Be Valiant

Children's Songbook p. 162

Opening Song: **Faith** *Children's Songbook* p. 96

Closing Song: **I Will Be Valiant** *Children's Songbook* p. 162

Materials Needed

- Picture of the Ten Virgins, if available
- Picture-book version of the fable "The Ant and the Grasshopper" by Amy Lowry Poole (or other version recommended by your local librarian)
- Copies of the included illustrations (2 each of "super ant" and ant pointing to self)
- 1 Piece of green construction paper
- 1 Piece of red construction paper
- Wooden paint-stirring stick or ruler
- Scissors
- Glue
- Black marker

Preparation

- Become familiar with the parable of the ten virgins (Matthew 25:1–13) and the story of the ant and the grasshopper.
- Color the illustrations.
- Cut the construction papers into octagons. Write "stop" on the red piece and "go" on the green piece.
- Glue the two signs together, back-to-back, with the paint stick in the middle as a handle.

Teaching Suggestions

Show the picture of the ten virgins (if a picture is not available, illustrate your story with simple drawings on the chalkboard) and briefly tell the story. Ask the children what they think this story relates to in the gospel and allow them to share their thoughts.

Next, show them the storybook and tell the children you have an additional story to tell them. It is not from the scriptures, but it has the same lesson. Read, or paraphrase, the fable of the ant and the grasshopper.

Tell the children that the song they will learn today talks about the kind of people Heavenly Father wants us to be like. Does He wants us to be wise or foolish virgins (wise) and would he prefer we be ants or grasshoppers (ants)? The song "I Will Be Valiant" tells us how to be good "serve-ants" for Heavenly Father.

Display each "serve-ant" picture and review the words that correspond to each. Try singing the song one time through.

Point out the rhythm of the music. It feels like something that should be marched to. Ask the children to stand quietly at their seats and march to the beat while singing the song one more time.

Next, show the stop and go sign. Have a reverent child come up and hold the sign on "go" while the children sing. At a point of his choice, he will stop the singing by turning the stop sign around. He will give the sign to another child who can correctly state the next few words in the song. Continue playing with the remaining time.

Close with a review of the story of the ten virgins. Emphasize your testimony of willingness to serve the Lord. Express the happiness that comes from choosing to be the Lord's "serve-ant".

WORDS AND CORRESPONDING PICTURES

- *The Lord needs valiant servants,* (super-ant)
- *To do his work in the latter day,* (ant working)
- *Who follow the teachings of Jesus* (ant with scriptures)
- *And serve his people in a loving way.* (ant giving service)
- *I will be his servant* (ant pointing to self)
- *And keep my conv'nants valiantly.* (super-ant)
- *I'll stand for truth. I'll stand for right.* (standing between truth and right)
- *The Lord can depend on me.* (ant pointing to self)

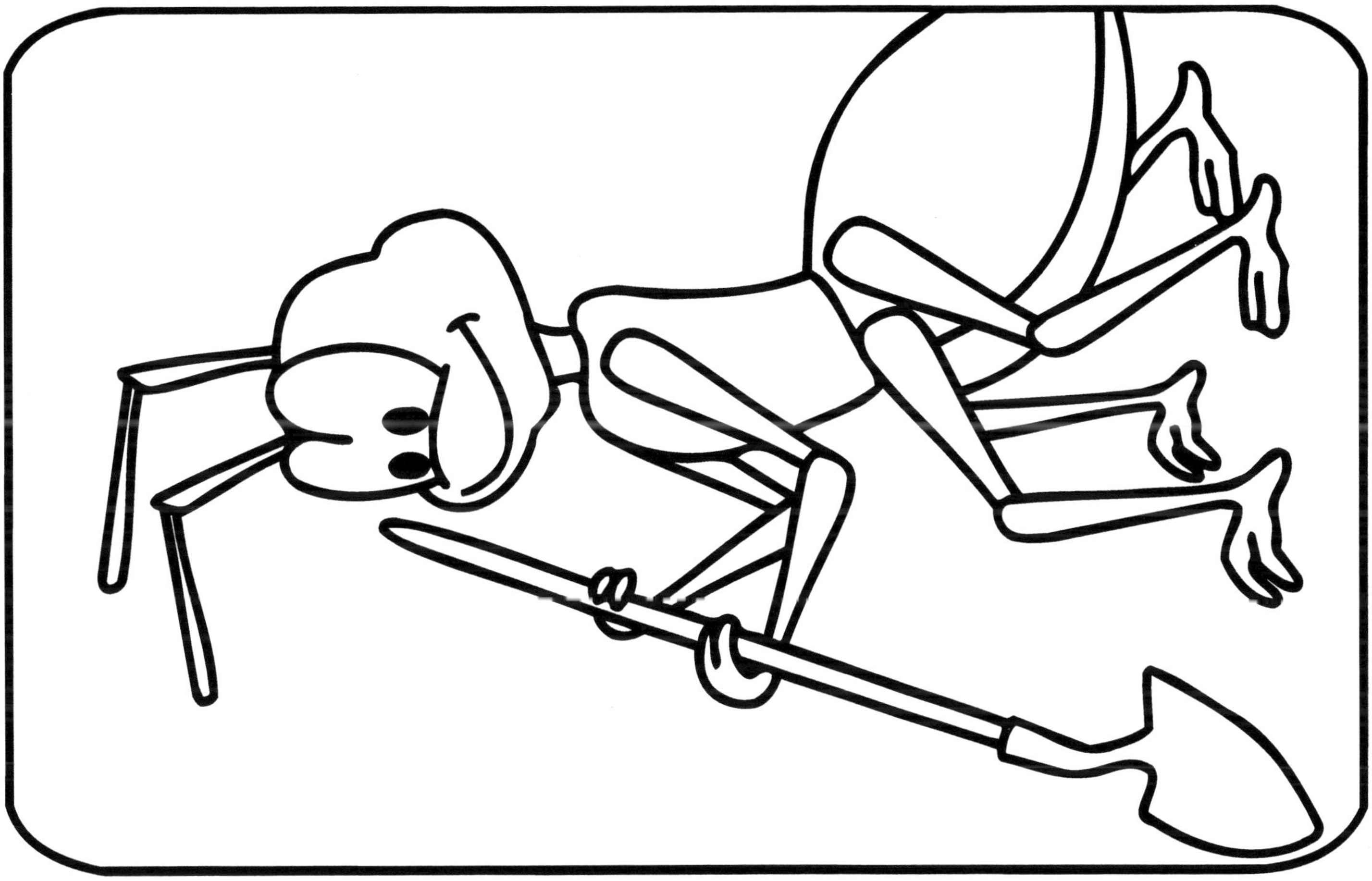

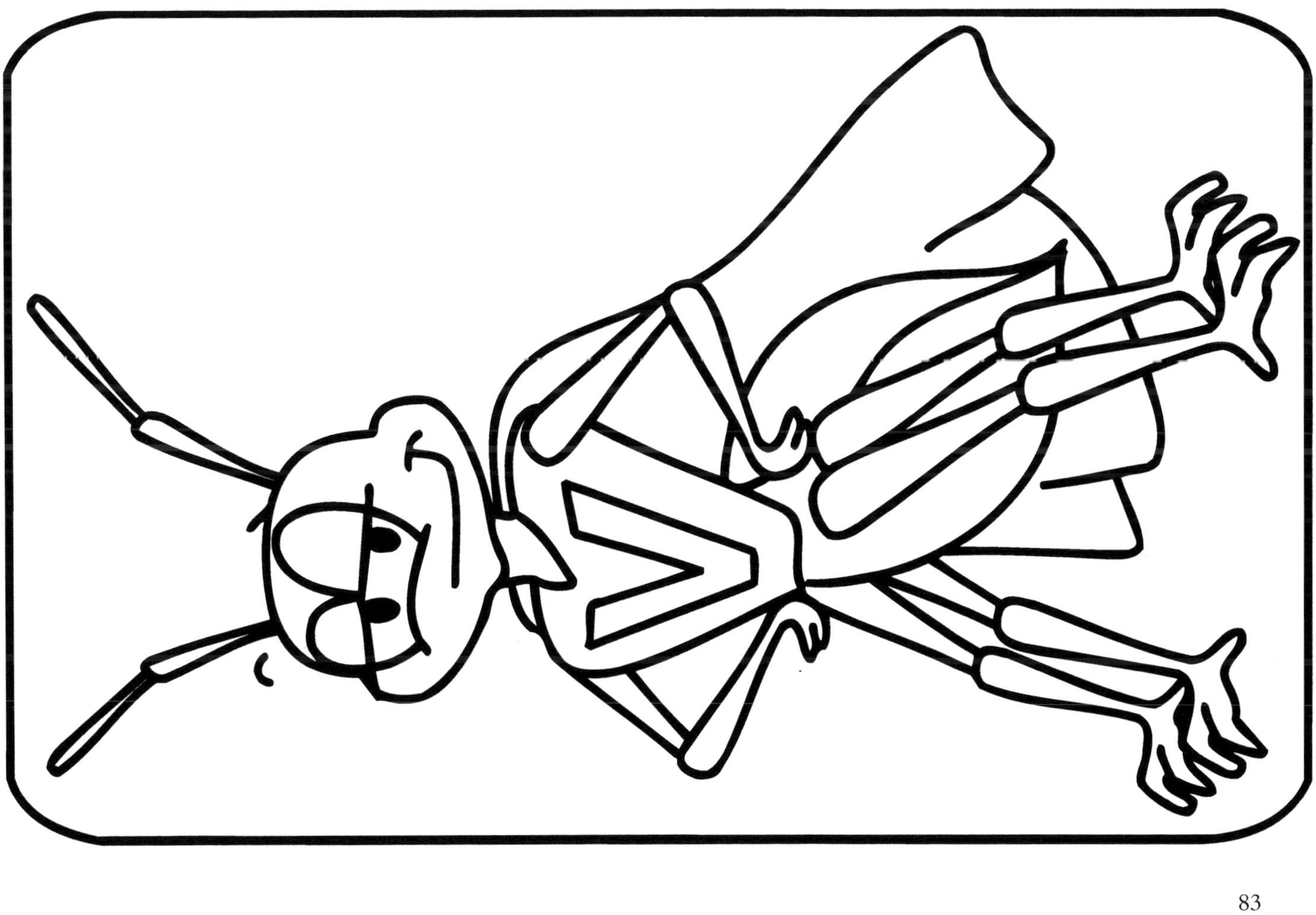

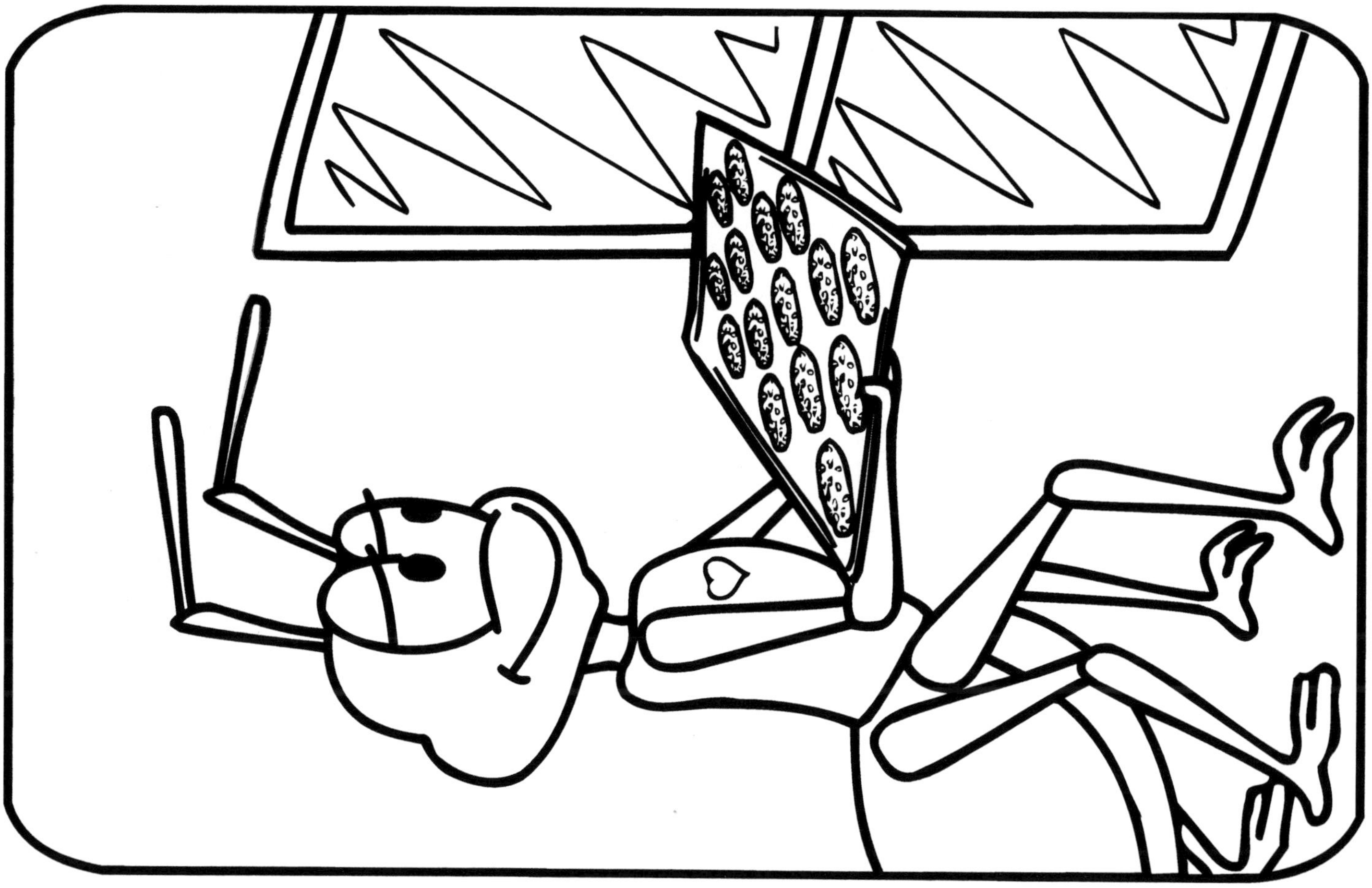

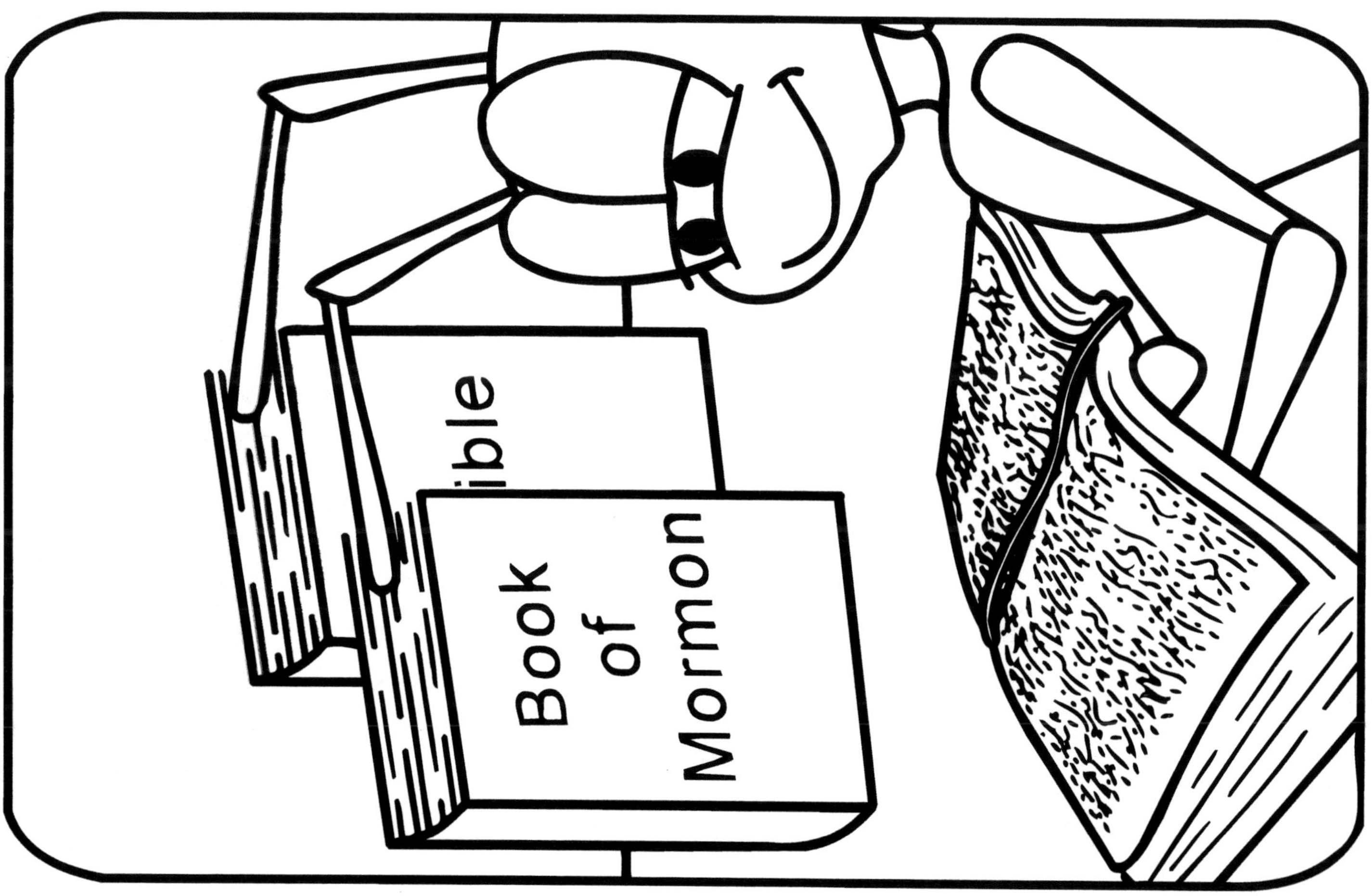
ible
Book
of
Mormon

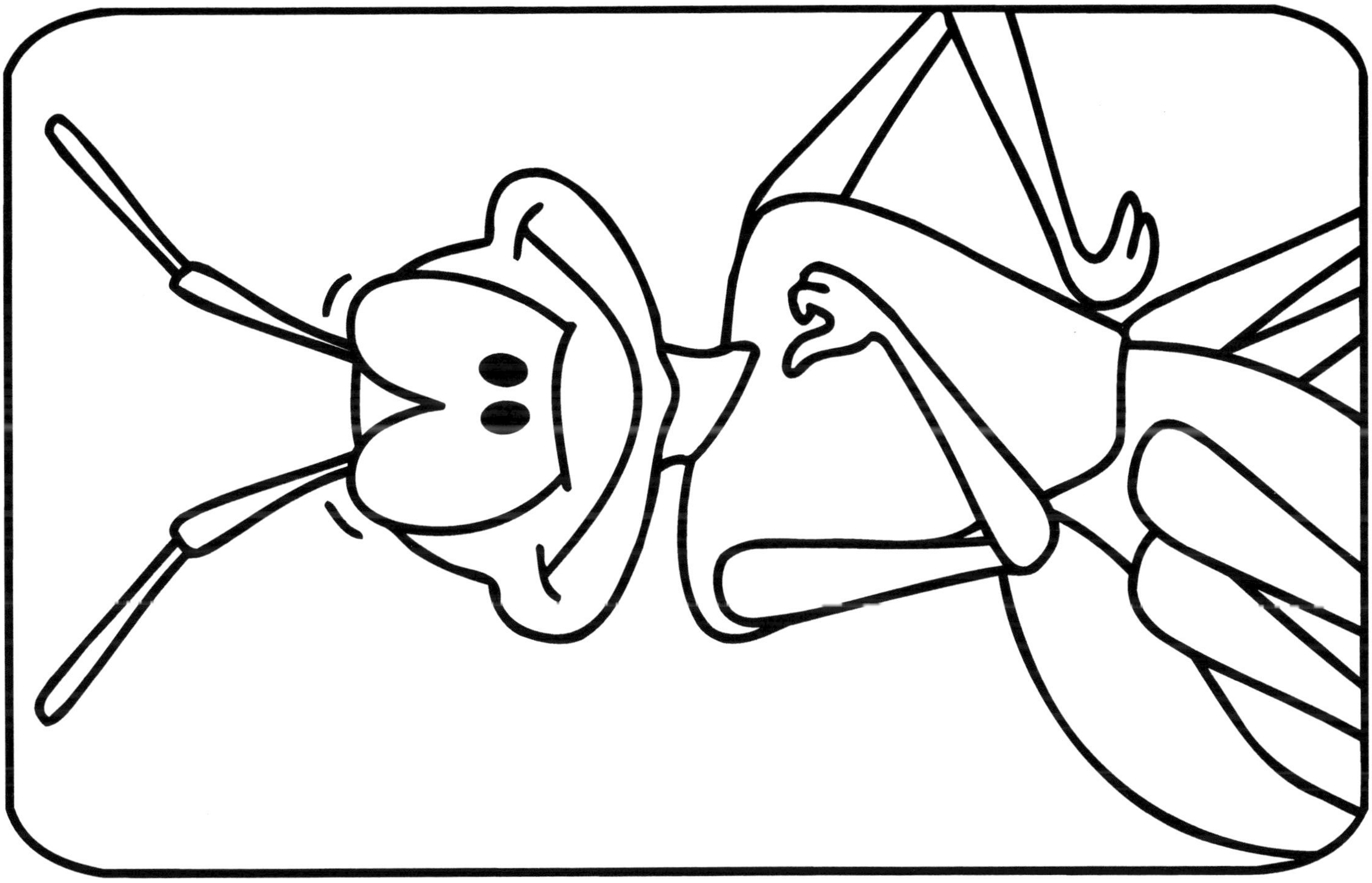

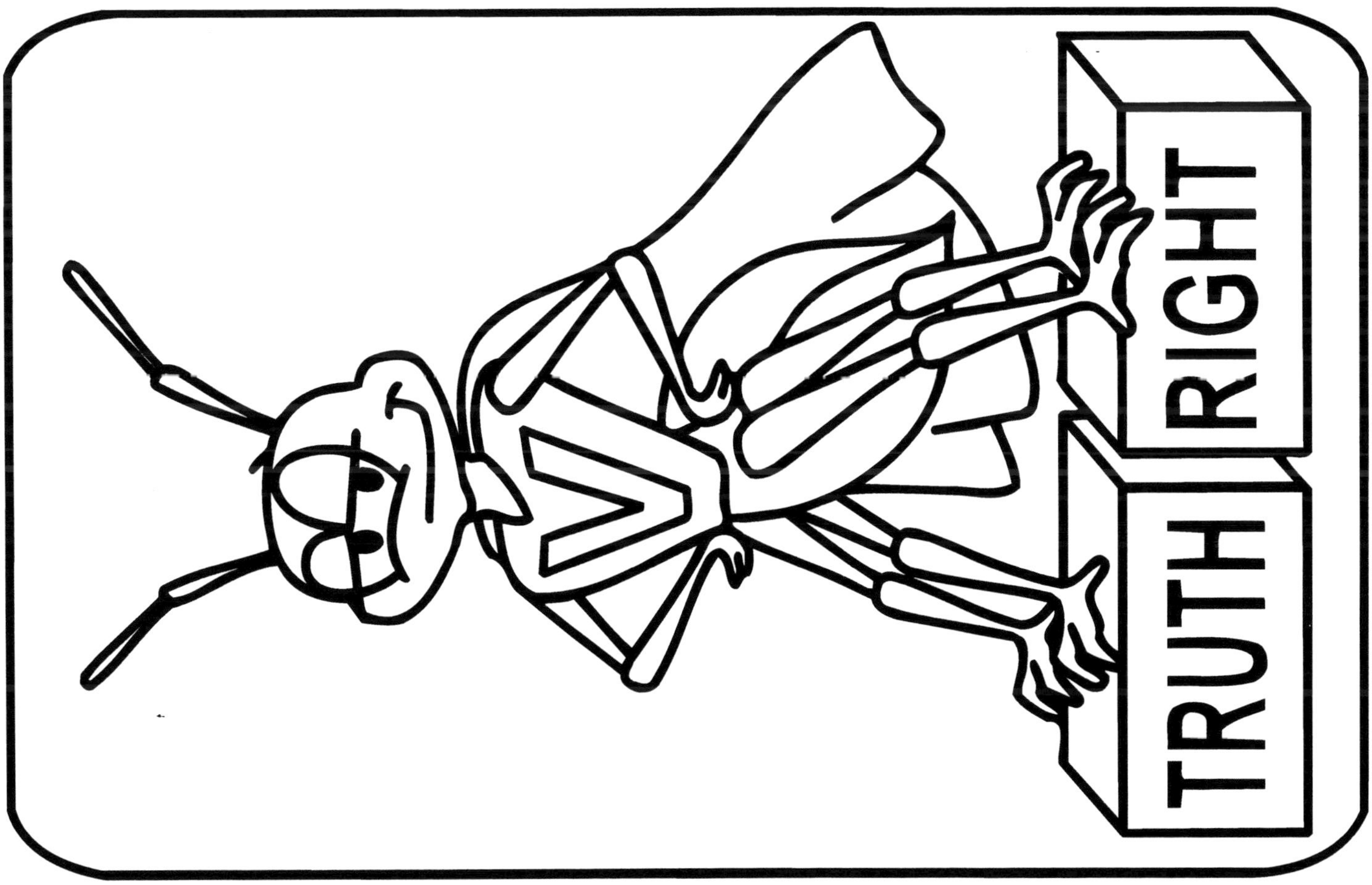
TRUTH
RIGHT

23. My Testimony

Based on the remarks of Sydney S. Reynolds at the special satellite broadcast for children, February 8, 2003.

Opening Song: **Faith** *Children's Songbook* p. 96

Closing Song: **The Holy Ghost** *Children's Songbook* p. 105

Materials Needed

- Copy of large hand
- Copies of the small hands for each child
- Crayons or colored pencils for use by the children
- Chalkboard or other display area
- Tape
- Scissors
- Stapler

Preparation

- Color each section of the large hand a different color.
- Cut the sections of the large hand apart.
- Cut the small hand sets apart on the lines and assemble them into small books. Staple them together down the left side like a book.

Teaching Suggestions

Tell the children that today they will be learning about testimonies.

As we learn and grow in the gospel, the Holy Ghost helps us to know that the things we are learning are true. These are the things that we have a testimony of. There are five things that are the building blocks for everything else we learn. They are the things we should learn to share with others when we bear our testimonies.

To help them remember what testimonies are, you will teach them to count off the basic principles on their hand: one through five.

Assemble your hand on the board a piece at a time. Briefly discuss each aspect and sing the corresponding song.

- **Heavenly Father**—Tell the children that the most basic thing they need to know is who God is. Ask the children to list some of the things they have learned about God. Help them to recognize the peaceful feeling they have as you discuss that God is our Heavenly Father, that we once lived with Him, and that we wanted to be like Him. Assist them in pointing out ways that we can see and feel each day that Heavenly Father loves us and wants us to be happy. **I Know My Father Lives** *Children's Songbook* p. 5.
- **Jesus Christ**—Because Heavenly Father loves us and knew there would be times we would make mistakes, He sent someone special to help us. He is our example and cleanses us from the things we do wrong and the hurts we feel. Jesus Christ is our special friend and brother, sent by Heavenly Father to show us how to return to Him. Jesus Christ is called our firm foundation. When we love Him and understand what He can do for us, this knowledge gives us the strength we need to choose the right. Once again, help the children recognize the feelings the Holy Ghost sends when you reverently talk about Jesus Christ. **I Believe in Christ** *Hymns* #134.
- **Joseph Smith**—Because Jesus Christ lived very long ago and His teachings got lost along the way, we needed someone who could help us know exactly what Jesus wanted us to know about His Church. Ask the children to tell you the story of a boy who knelt in a grove of trees to find out which church he should join. Help the children complete this story, including the coming forth of the Book of Mormon (See Joseph Smith-History). Remind them that because of these events, we know exactly what Jesus wants us to be like. **On a Golden Springtime,** verse 3 *Children's Songbook* p. 88.
- **True Church**—Because Joseph Smith restored the truth and translated the Book of Mormon we can be members of Christ's true church today. It's just like the church that Jesus established when He came to earth. This Church is the same no matter where you go because Christ is at its head. **The Church of Jesus Christ** *Children's Songbook* p. 77.
- **Living Prophet**—Assure the children that even though Jesus Christ is not here with us today, He would never leave us without someone to look to for answers. A prophet, called by God, speaks for Him and helps us to always know how we can be more like Heavenly Father. Ask the children to list some of the things the prophets have told us we need to do. **Latter-day Prophets** *Children's Songbook* p. 134.

After your discussion, present the children with the testimony books. Allow them to color and illustrate their books with their own testimonies.

SPECIAL NOTE

- For a discussion on helping children to know when to bear their testimony refer to: Carl B. Cook, "When Children Want to Bear Testimony," *Ensign*, December 2002, p. 29.

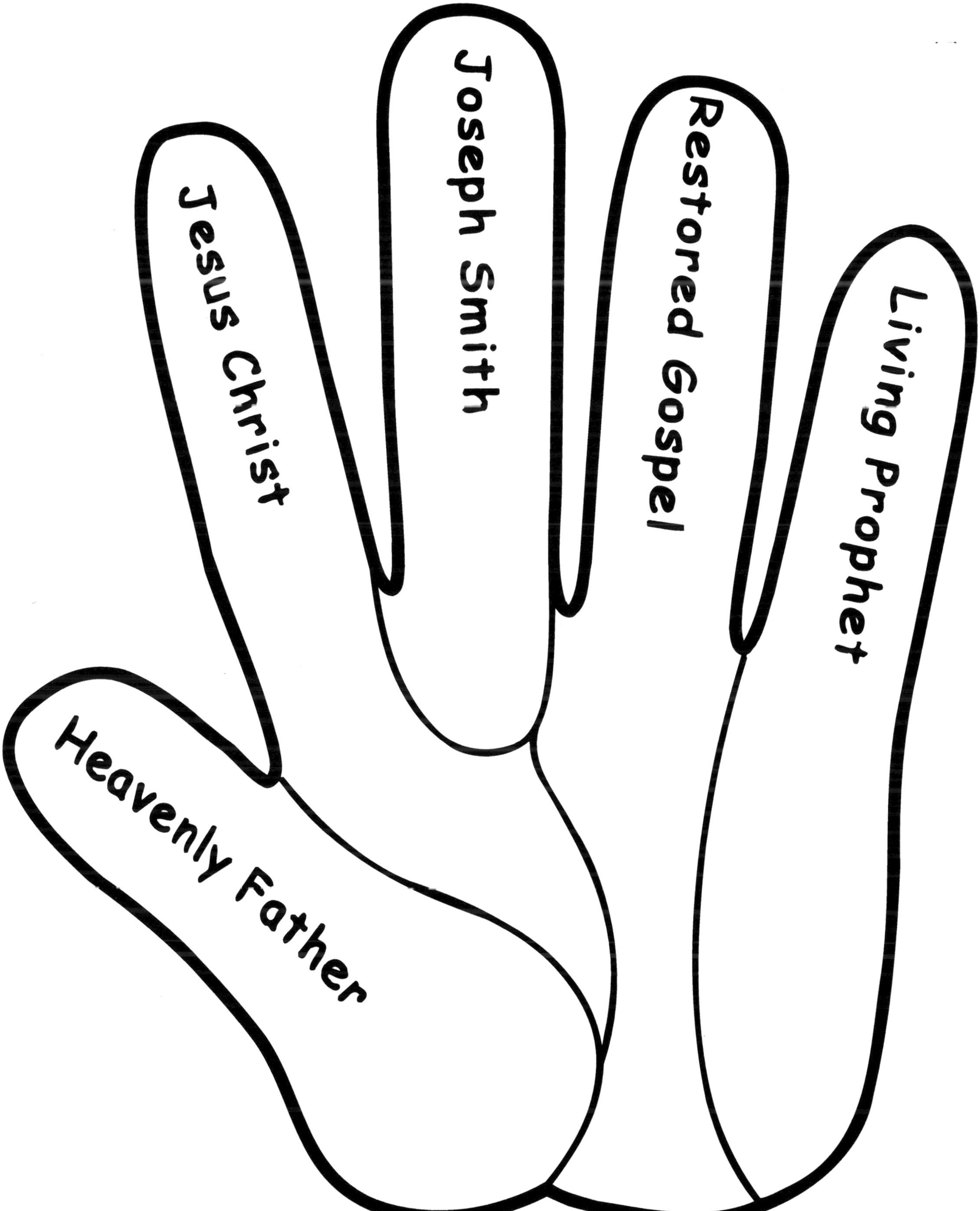
Heavenly Father
Jesus Christ
Joseph Smith
Restored Gospel
Living Prophet

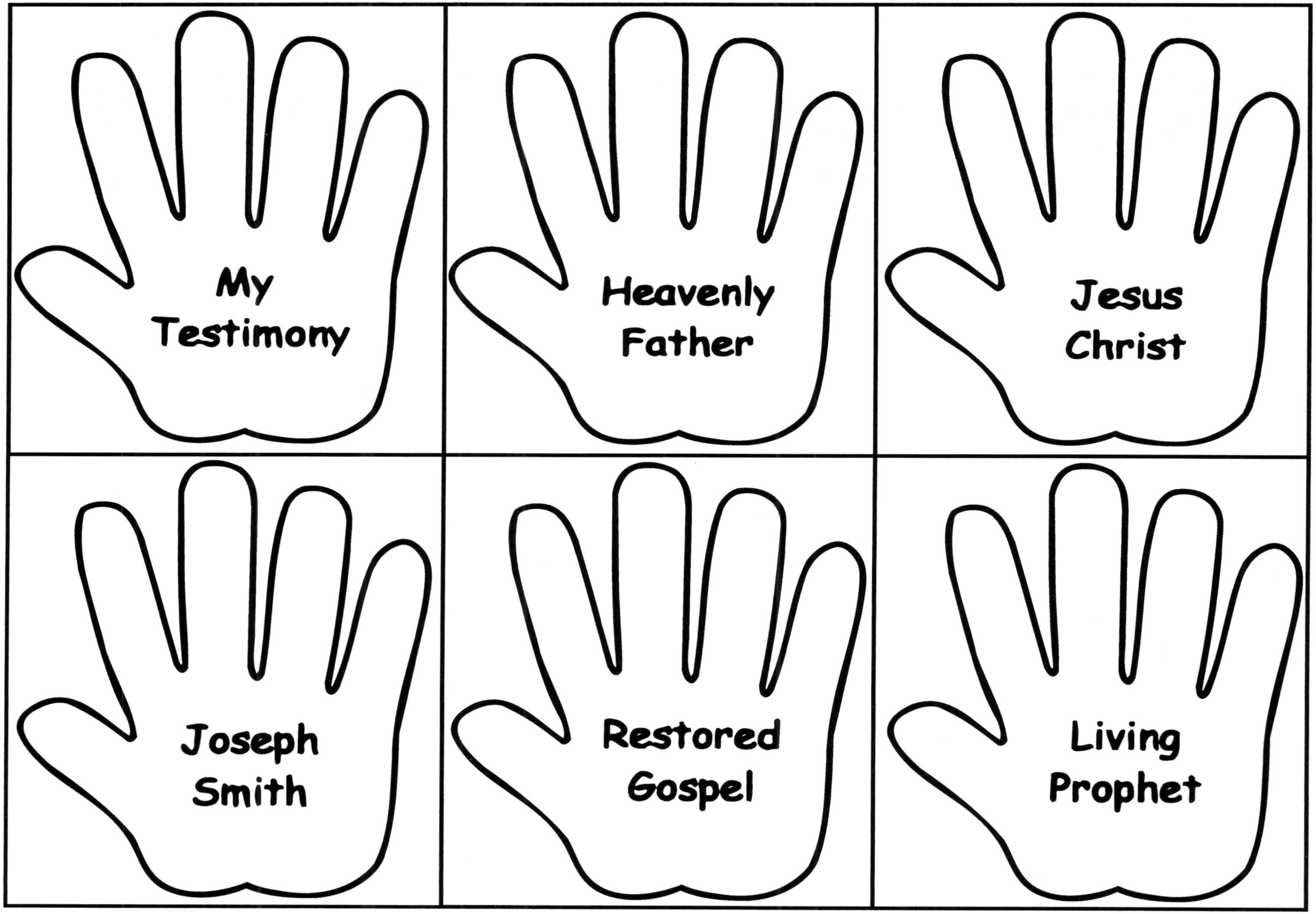
My Testimony
Heavenly Father
Jesus Christ
Joseph Smith
Restored Gospel
Living Prophet

24. I Want to Live the Gospel

Children's Songbook p. 148

Opening Song: **I Will Be Valiant** *Children's Songbook* p. 162

Closing Song: **I Want to Live the Gospel** *Children's Songbook* p. 148

Materials Needed

- 11 Sheets of construction paper (1 white, 2 each of 5 other colors)
- 5 Sheets of white paper
- Small square box with all 6 sides present
- Clear packing tape
- Chalkboard or other display area
- Large individual letters to spell "I Want to Live the Gospel"
- Tape
- Scissors

Preparation

- Tape the box closed.
- Cut 1 of each color of construction paper to cover the sides of the box, and tape them in place with the clear packing tape.
- Write one of the five phrases of the song on each piece of white paper, and back them with the rest of the colored construction paper.
- Write the True/False statements on the back of each letter.
- Tape the letters, in order of the title, across the bottom of the chalkboard.
- Tape the song phrases down the middle of the chalkboard, with the chorus sheet after the first verse.

Teaching Suggestions

Ask the children to tell you about the things they have been learning this past year. Let them share their thoughts with you. Tell them that you are very proud of them for all the things they have learned and how they are trying to live the gospel.

Tell them that the song they will learn today is about living the gospel. Introduce the title and words to the song by pointing them out on the board. Read each set of words; let the children repeat it with you, then sing each phrase one time with the piano.

To help the children practice this song they will choose letters from the title of the song. On the back of each will be a statement about something they have learned this year. They have to decide if what the statement says is true, or false. If they answer correctly, have the child gently roll the colored cube you created.

Whatever color side turns up is the portion of the song you will review again. Repeat the words with the children, and then sing it. If the cube lands on the white side, sing the whole song one time through. After the words have been reviewed the second time through, turn the words over and see if they can say the phrase from memory when it comes around again.

Close with your testimony and a challenge for the children to choose one thing they learned to try to do better and follow Heavenly Father's plan for them.

SONG PHRASING

- *I want to live the gospel, To know that its teachings are true,*
- *To follow the plan of my Savior And live as he wants me to do.*
- *I will try in all I do and say To live the gospel more each day.* (write it once, but be sure to sing it twice for each chorus)
- *I want to live the gospel, To know I am hear when I pray,*
- *To know that I will be happy Because I have learned to obey.*

TRUE/FALSE STATEMENTS

- Joseph Smith was born in 1980.
- Adam and Eve still live in the Garden of Eden.
- As part of His plan, Heavenly Father provided a Savior so we could live with Him again.
- I came to earth to play video games.
- Jesus Christ atoned for my sins.
- Jesus was never baptized.
- I can pray and receive answers to my prayers.
- I don't have to be nice to my family.
- The Priesthood was restored after the Book of Mormon was published.
- There are twelve Articles of Faith.
- Faith in Jesus Christ grows as we learn about Him and try to choose the right.
- A testimony has five important parts.
- I can be baptized when I turn seven.
- When I am confirmed, I receive the gift of the Holy Ghost.
- I take the sacrament to remember my baptismal covenants.
- Agency means reading your scriptures.

- When I keep the commandments, I show Heavenly Father I love Him.
- My body is a temple.
- Heavenly Father's plan teaches me how to be happy.
- I didn't want to follow Heavenly Father's plan in the premortal existence.

25. I Am Thankful for Jesus Christ

Opening Song: **I Believe in Christ** *Hymns* # 134

Closing Song: **When He Comes Again** *Children's Songbook* p. 82

Materials Needed

- Plain wrapping paper and ribbon
- Half sheets of white paper, one for each child
- Crayons or colored pencils for use by the children
- Large Christmas stocking
- A few small items that represent gifts Christ has given us. (Ideas are given at the end of this lesson.)
- Blank gift tags

Preparation

- Decorate your Primary bulletin board, or other appropriate display area, to look like a large present.
- Place a gift tag on each small item representing the gifts of Christ. Label the tag with a song from the *Children's Songbook*.
- Place the items into the stocking.

Teaching Suggestions

Explain to the children that they will be looking at gifts Christ has given us. Reverent children will come forward and draw an item from your stocking. Briefly describe what it symbolizes, and then sing the corresponding song.

Next, have the children draw a picture of a gift they can give to Christ in return. Post these on the gift box bulletin board for display during the remainder of the month.

Remember to close with your testimony and your gratitude for all the children have learned over the last year.

POSSIBLE ITEMS AND SONGS

- **Silk flower** (creation and nature) **Beauty Everywhere** *Children's Songbook* p. 232
- **Scriptures** (instructions for how to live) **Seek the Lord Early** *Children's Songbook* p. 108
- **Picture of family** (family that loves me) **Love Is Spoken Here** *Children's Songbook* p. 190
- **Bar of soap** (atonement to cleanse me from sin) **He Sent His Son** *Children's Songbook* p. 34
- **Ward bulletin** (restored church) **The Church of Jesus Christ** *Children's Songbook* p. 77
- **Small picture of a temple** (temples to learn more about Him and how to get back to Heavenly Father) **I Love to See the Temple** *Children's Songbook* p. 95
- **Sacrament cup** (Sacrament to help us remember our covenants) **To Think about Jesus** *Children's Songbook* p. 71

About the Author

Alison Palmer is a life-long member of The Church of Jesus Christ of Latter-day Saints. Born in Mesa, Arizona, she grew up in West Virginia and graduated from Marshall University with a bachelor's degree in Nursing. Alison stopped practicing nursing after several years, to raise and home school her children.

Over the years, Alison has held many callings in the Church, including several that have helped develop her great love for the Primary children. She has served as nursery leader, pianist, chorister, teacher, den leader and Primary president. She has also been spotted teaching Sunday School, serving as a teacher or leader in Relief Society, and occasionally braving girl's camp.

Writing is Alison's favorite pastime, but you can also find her lost within the pages of a good book, playing piano, cooking, attending the temple, taking long walks, sewing, or playing with her family. She feels her greatest accomplishments come from the dynamic rewards of raising children who are trying to live righteously.

Other works by Alison Palmer which Horizon Publishers has produced include: *Planting Seeds of Faith: Fun Character-Building Activities for LDS Children* and *Walking the Path of Faith: More Fun Character-Building Activities for LDS Children.*

The Palmers currently reside in Michigan.

9 26575 07808 7

I Feel My Savior's Love

Themes from LDS Children's Songs in Counted Cross-Stitch

Contents

Sharalee S. Clawson

Barbara K. Marshall

Instructions

Choose your material. Cut a piece 6 to 8 inches larger than the finished size of the design. Whip the edges of the fabric, or fold masking tape over the raw edges to prevent unraveling. A fray-check solution also can be used.

The center of each design is found by following the vertical and horizontal centering arrows until they meet in the middle. This is the beginning point on the graph. All work should be counted from this point out.

Center the fabric on a hoop. Pull the material taut and screw the hoop tightly. Use two strands of thread with 14-count cloth.

Do not knot the thread. Leave a 2-inch tail as you pull the thread through the material for the first time. As you begin stitching, catch the tail at the back in the stitches. When the thread is nearly gone, slip the needle and thread under a few stitches and clip off the thread.

All stitches should cross in the same direction to give the design a smooth look. If the bottom half of the cross-stitches are done from lower left to upper right, the top stitches are done from upper left to lower right. When stitching a one-color area, stitch the diagonal bottom of each square across an entire row, and then return doing the top diagonal of each stitch. (See Figure 1.)

In order to give shape and stronger definition to the facial features and a few other parts, a quarter stitch is used. This is done by bringing the needle up through one hole and down through the middle of the square. (See Figure 2.) In some patterns there will be a quarter stitch in one color and a quarter stitch in another color in the same square. The backstitch color is usually the top cross-stitch of the square.

The backstitch is generally done last to outline the figure and give dimension to the piece. Place the needle down in the hole behind the first stitch, then work one stitch back on top of the fabric and two stitches forward beneath the fabric to form a solid line. (See Figure 3.)

After stitching is completed, hand wash the finished piece with mild soap. Handle it gently and rinse it thoroughly. Do not wring out the water. Pat the piece between the layers of a dry towel to absorb the excess moisture. Then place it on a dry towel, floss side down. To press an Aida-cloth sampler, use an iron adjusted for the "cotton" setting. Some other fabrics may require a cooler setting.

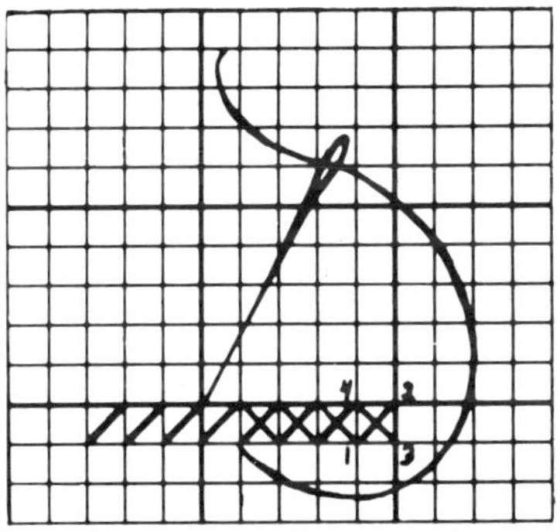

Figure 1
Basic Cross-Stitch

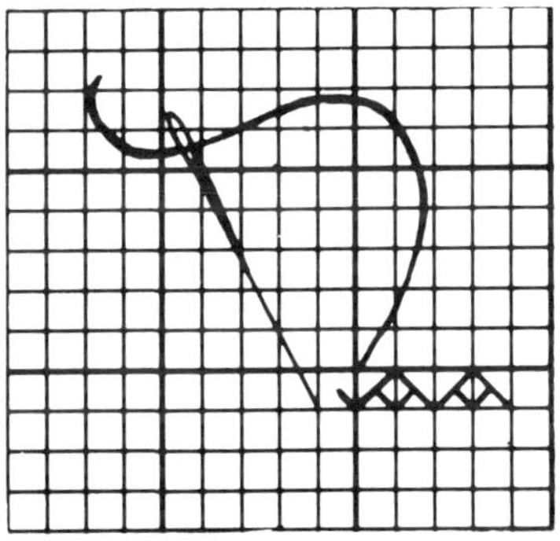

Figure 2
Quarter Stitch

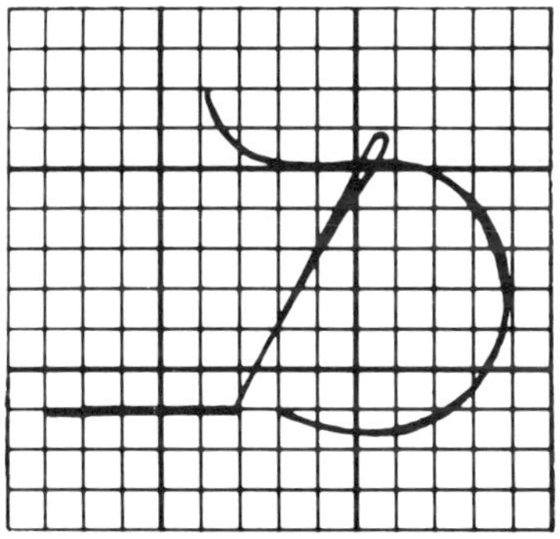

Figure 3
Backstitch Outline

Stitch Count

		90	95	100	105	110	115	120	125	130	135	140	145	150	155	160	165	170	175	180	185	190
Thread	**11**	8¼	8⅝	9⅛	9½	10	10½	10⅞	11⅜	11⅞	12¼	12¾	13¼	13⅝	14⅛	14½	15	15½	15⅞	16⅜	16¾	17¼
Count	**14**	6½	6¾	7⅛	7½	7⅞	8¼	8⅝	8⅞	9¼	9⅝	10	10⅜	10¾	11⅛	11⅜	11⅞	12⅛	12½	12⅞	13¼	13½
per	**18**	5	5¼	5½	5⅞	6⅛	6⅜	6⅝	7	7¼	7½	7¾	8	8⅜	8⅝	8⅞	9⅛	9⅜	9¾	10	10¼	10½
Inch	**22**	4⅛	4⅜	4½	4¾	5	5¼	5½	5⅝	5⅞	6⅛	6⅜	6½	6⅜	7	7¼	7½	7¾	8	8⅛	8⅜	8½

Using the information given with individual patterns, determine the design area of your sampler by finding the point on the chart where the stitch count intersects with the thread count, per inch of the fabric used. An additional 6 to 8 inches should be added for margin areas.

Embroidery Hoop Framing

Mounting the Sampler into the Hoop

Select a quality wooden or plastic embroidery hoop with a screw tension adjustment. It should be large enough to accommodate the sampler design comfortably.

Place the sampler on a flat surface, design up, and position the hoop on the fabric so the design is centered, with the tension screw placed at the center top. You may wish to count blank squares to accurately center the design. Mark and cut the fabric in a square so the edges extend 1½ to 2 inches beyond the hoop at the narrowest points. (See Figure 4.) Use the same dimensions to cut a piece of broadcloth for backing. It should be the same color as the sampler fabric.

Stretch both the sampler and backing carefully onto the hoop, keeping the design centered. Make tension adjustments, as necessary, until the fabrics are smooth and tight.

Place the hoop with the sampler face down and apply glue, sparingly, to the top edge of the inner ring of the embroidery hoop. Do this in short, manageable intervals, pulling only the excess backing fabric over the glued edge of the hoop and holding it in place until the fabric is secure. Repeat this procedure with the sampler fabric, gluing it to the backing fabric along the inner ring of the embroidery hoop. (See Figure 5.) We suggest using a hot-melt (glue gun) glue. The excess Aida cloth and backing fabric can now be trimmed away if desired.

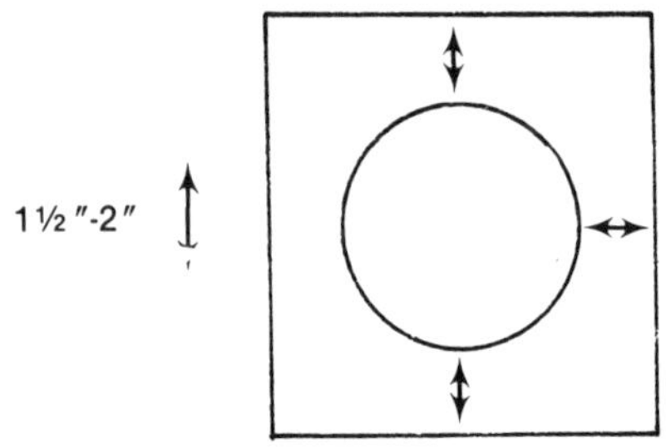

Figure 4

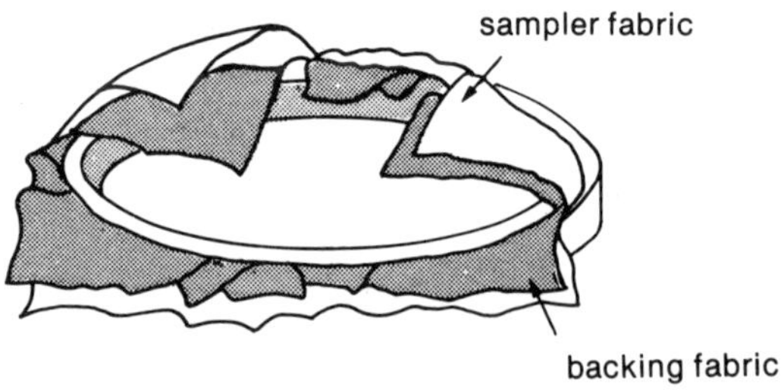

Figure 5

Attaching the Ruffle and Lace

With the sampler still face down, carefully apply glue to the top edge of the outer ring of the embroidery hoop and secure a pre-gathered lace in place around the circumference of the hoop. (See Figure 6.) The lace should be long enough to reach around the hoop easily.

To add a cloth ruffle, cut a 4-inch-wide strip of fabric to a length equaling twice the circumference of the embroidery hoop. With right sides together, sew the ends of the fabric strip together. Open and press the seam flat. Fold this "ring" of material in half lengthwise, with raw edges together and right sides out, to form a 2-inch strip. Press it.

Place a length of heavy crochet thread along the raw edge of the ruffle strip about ¼-inch from the edge, and zig-zag over the top of the thread. This thread should be slightly longer than the ruffle strip and knotted at both ends so the ends will not pull through the zig-zag stitch. (See Figure 7.) Use this thread as a drawstring to gather the ruffle to correspond with the size of the hoop. Glue the cloth ruffle to the outer ring of the embroidery hoop directly on top of the lace. (See Figure 6.) On the finished side, a ribbon can be glued (use white craft glue) to the outside edge of the embroidery hoop. A bow can be secured over the tension screw. (See cover photo.)

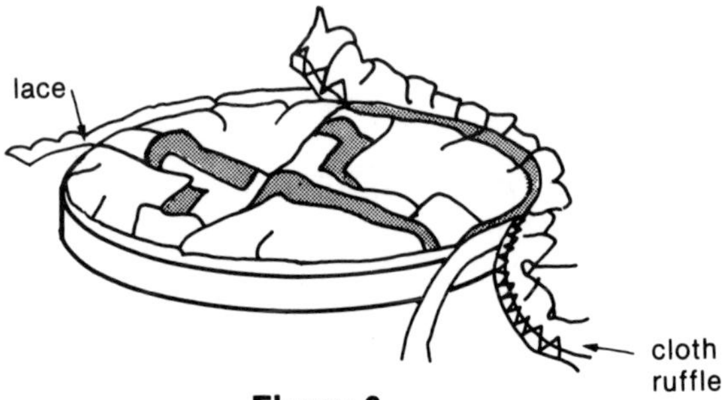

Figure 6

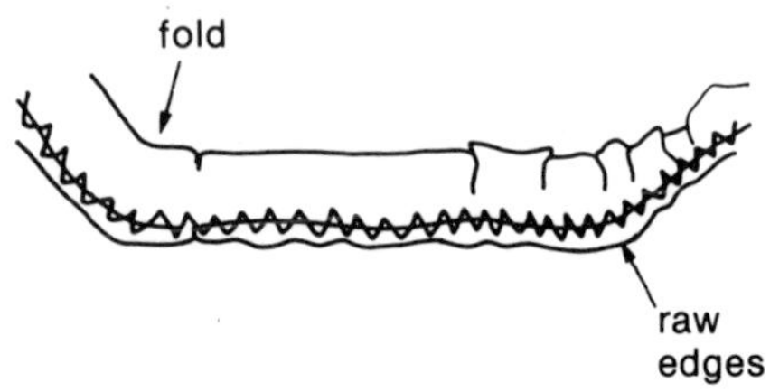

Figure 7

I Feel My Savior's Love in All the World Around Me

•Shaded rows are a repeat of the last two rows of the other half of the chart.

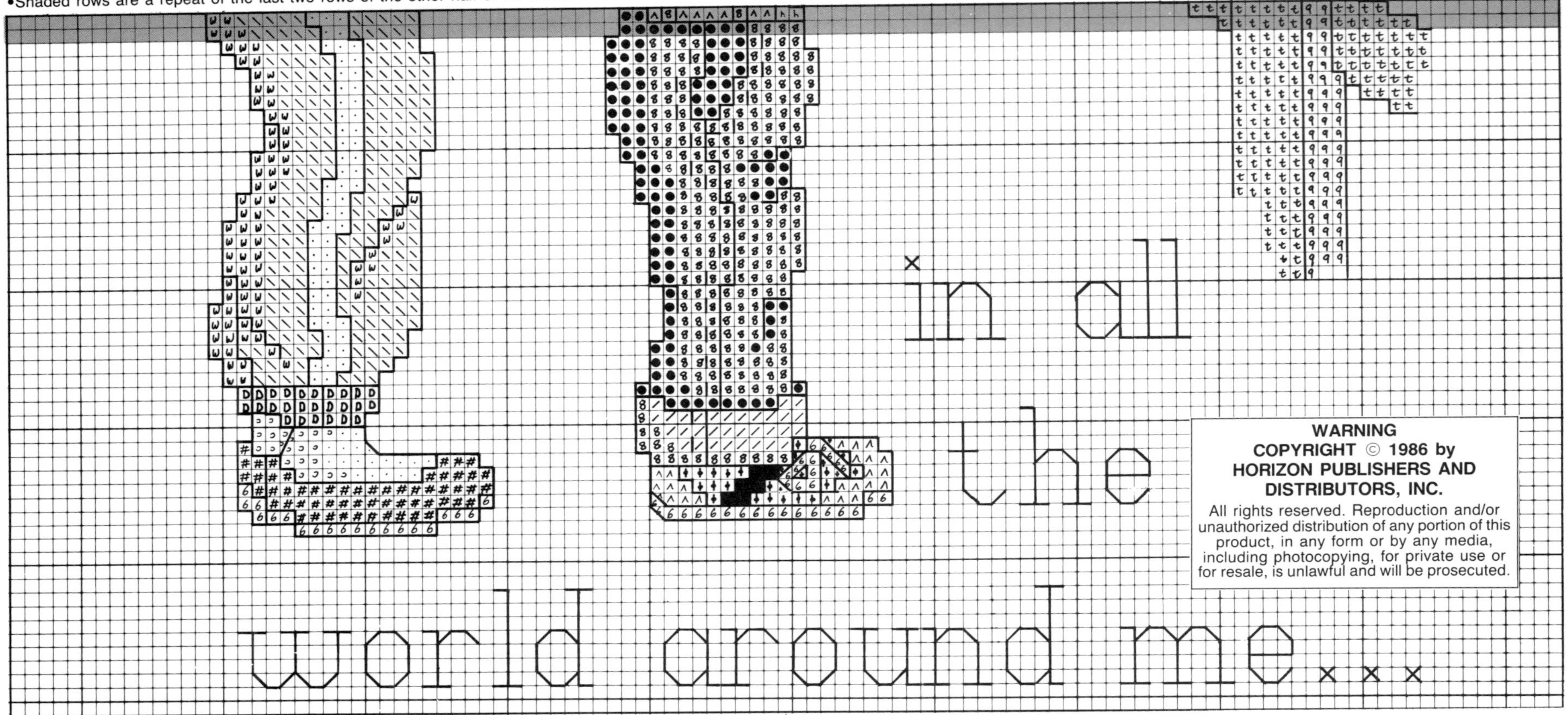

The design area is 131 x 107; 9 3/8" × 7 3/4" on 14-count Aida cloth.

The model is stitched on white 14-count Aida cloth.

Symbol	DMC	Color Description
6	739	beige
ε	738	tan, very light
♦	437	tan, light
■	801	brown, dark
•	blanc neige	white
–	754	peach, light
c	353	peach, medium
ɔ	762	pearl gray, light
\	818	baby pink
ω	776	pink, medium

Symbol	DMC	Color Description
D	899	rose, medium
#	844	beaver gray, very dark
∧	435	brown, very light
T	966	baby green
0	368	pistachio green, light
●	320	pistachio green, medium
h	727	topaz yellow, light
/	932	antique blue, light
8	931	antique blue, medium

Symbol	DMC	Color Description
●	930	antique blue, dark
t	3024	brown gray, very light
q	3023	brown gray, light
N	472	avocado green, light
0	471	avocado green, medium
e	612	drab brown, medium
ll	611	drab brown, dark
⁄	519	sky blue
——	470	avocado green
——	801	brown, dark

The veins in the leaves are backstitched with two strands DMC #470.
The words are backstitched with two strands DMC #801.
The stems on the tree are backstitched with two strands DMC #801.
The bird's eye is a french knot done with DMC #801.
All other backstitching is done with one strand DMC #801.

I Hope They Call Me on a Mission

•Shaded rows are a repeat of the last two rows of the other half of the chart

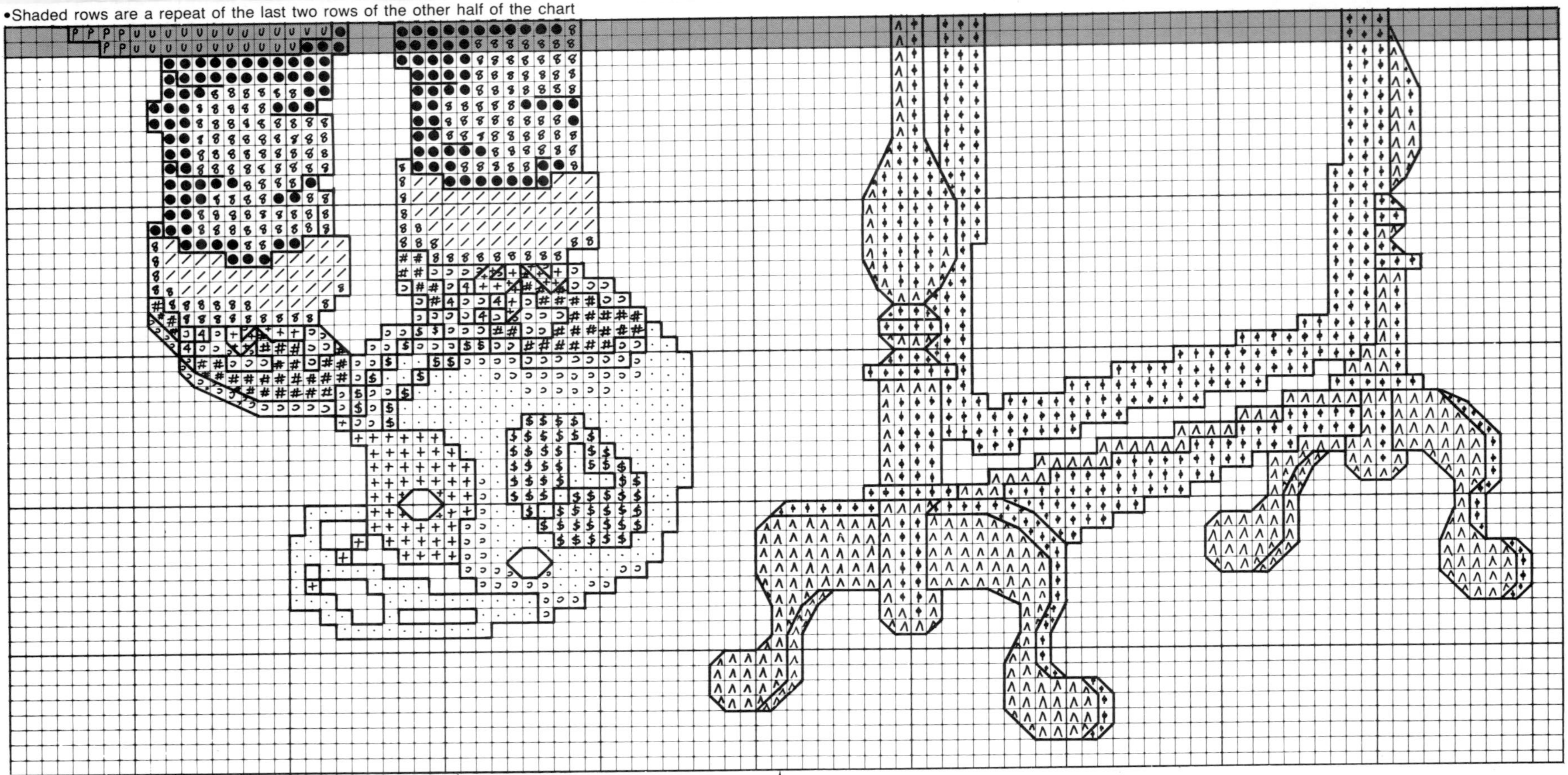

The design area is 96 × 126 squares; 6¾″ × 9″ on 14-count Aida cloth.

The model is stitched on cream 14-count Aida cloth.

Symbol	DMC	Color Description
⌐	3047	yellow beige, light
v	3046	yellow beige, medium
–	754	peach, light
c	353	peach, medium
•	blanc neige	white
$	312	blue, dark
ɔ	762	pearl gray, light

Symbol	DMC	Color Description
d	501	blue green, dark
↘	840	beige brown, medium
P	839	beige brown, dark
▼	838	beige brown, very dark
/	932	antique blue, light
8	931	antique blue, medium
●	930	antique blue, dark

Symbol	DMC	Color Description
#	844	beaver gray, very dark
⬮	645	beaver gray, dark
4	725	topaz
+	318	steel gray
♦	437	tan, light
∧	435	brown, very light
——	801	brown, dark
——	3371	black brown

The suit coat is backstitched outside and inside with one strand DMC #3371.
The swivel pin in the mirror is backstitched with two strands DMC #801.
The words are backstitched with two strands DMC #801.
All other backstitching is done with one strand DMC #801.

I Love to See the Temple

Symbol	DMC	Color Description
I	783	christmas gold
ꟼ	782	topaz, medium
Γ	677	antique gold, light
v	3046	yellow beige, medium
:	951	flesh, light
2	945	flesn
y	211	lavender
//	210	lavender, medium
¢	209	lavender, dark
•	blanc neige	white
∧	435	brown, very light
z	436	tan
⋰	964	aqua, light
=	959	aqua, medium

Symbol	DMC	Color Description
⁄	958	aqua, dark
ɔ	762	pearl gray, light
>	452	shell gray, medium
——	452	shell gray, medium
——	783	christmas gold
- - - -	451	shell gray, dark
——	801	brown, dark

The golden window and angel are backstitched with two strands DMC #783.

The words are backstitched with two strands DMC #801.

The temple is backstitched with two colors. The regular backstitch lines are backstitched with two strands DMC #452. The lines marked with - - - are backstitched with two strands DMC #451.

All other backstitching is done with one strand DMC #801.

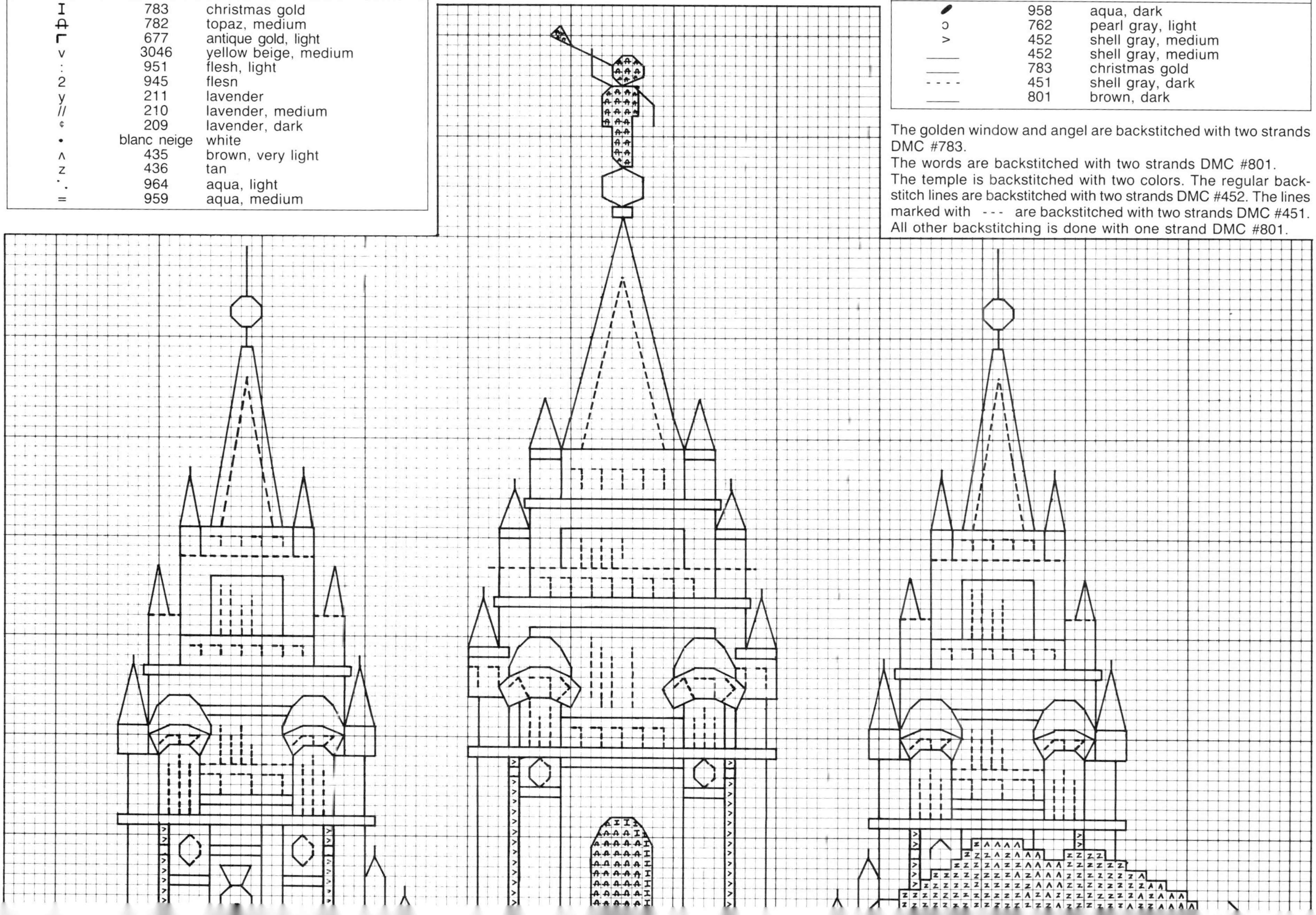

The design area is 123x189; $8^5/_8$″x$13^1/_2$″ on 14-count Aida cloth.

The model is stitched on cream 14-count Aida cloth.

Family Night is Always Fun

The design area is 121x89; 8⅔″ × 6⅓″ on 14-count Aida cloth.

•Shaded rows are a repeat of the last two rows of the other half of the chart.

The model is stitched on cream 14-count Aida cloth.

Symbol	DMC	Color Description
o	301	mahogany, medium
◥	400	mahogany, dark
–	754	peach, light
c	353	peach, medium
•	blanc neige	white
●	930	antique blue, dark
7	350	coral, medium
.·	3042	antique violet, light
◆	3041	antique violet, medium
ɔ	762	pearl gray, light
• •	746	off white
Γ	3047	yellow beige, light
4	725	topaz
⍀	415	pearl gray
+	318	steel gray
x	422	hazelnut brown, light
∪	3045	yellow beige, dark
6	739	beige
ε	738	tan, very light
♦	437	tan, light
E	722	bittersweet, medium
/	932	antique blue, light
8	931	antique blue, medium
●●	413	pewter gray, dark
⌋	ecru	antique white
z	436	tan
■	801	brown, dark
I	3072	beaver gray, very light
ℓ	648	beaver gray, light
B	647	beaver gray, medium
▲	3362	loden green, dark
———	930	antique blue, dark
———	801	brown, dark

The narrow stripe in the bowl is done with one strand DMC #930.

The words are backstitched with two strands DMC #801.

All other backstitching is done with one strand DMC #801.

The Temple Gates

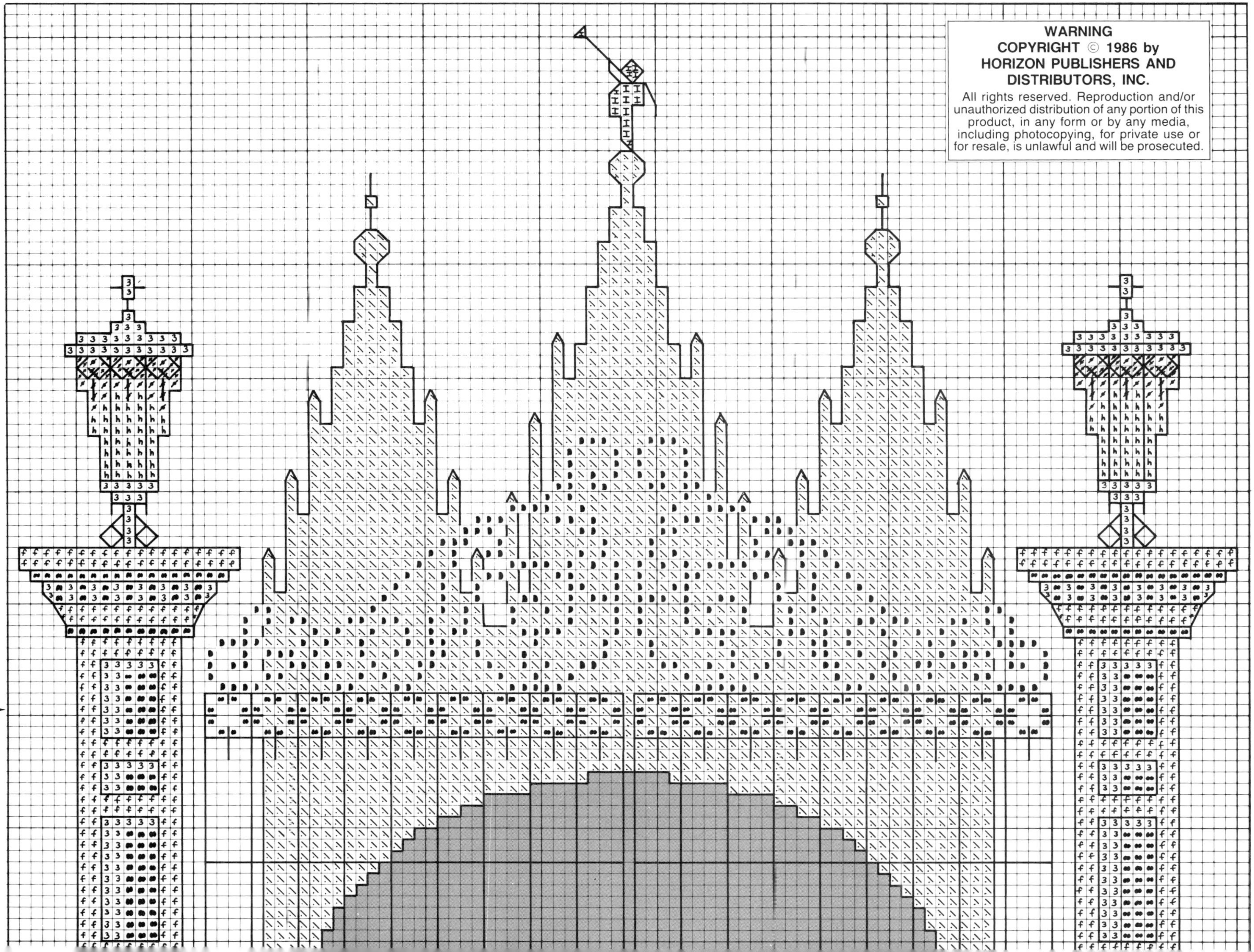

•Shaded rows are a repeat of the last two rows of the other half of the chart.

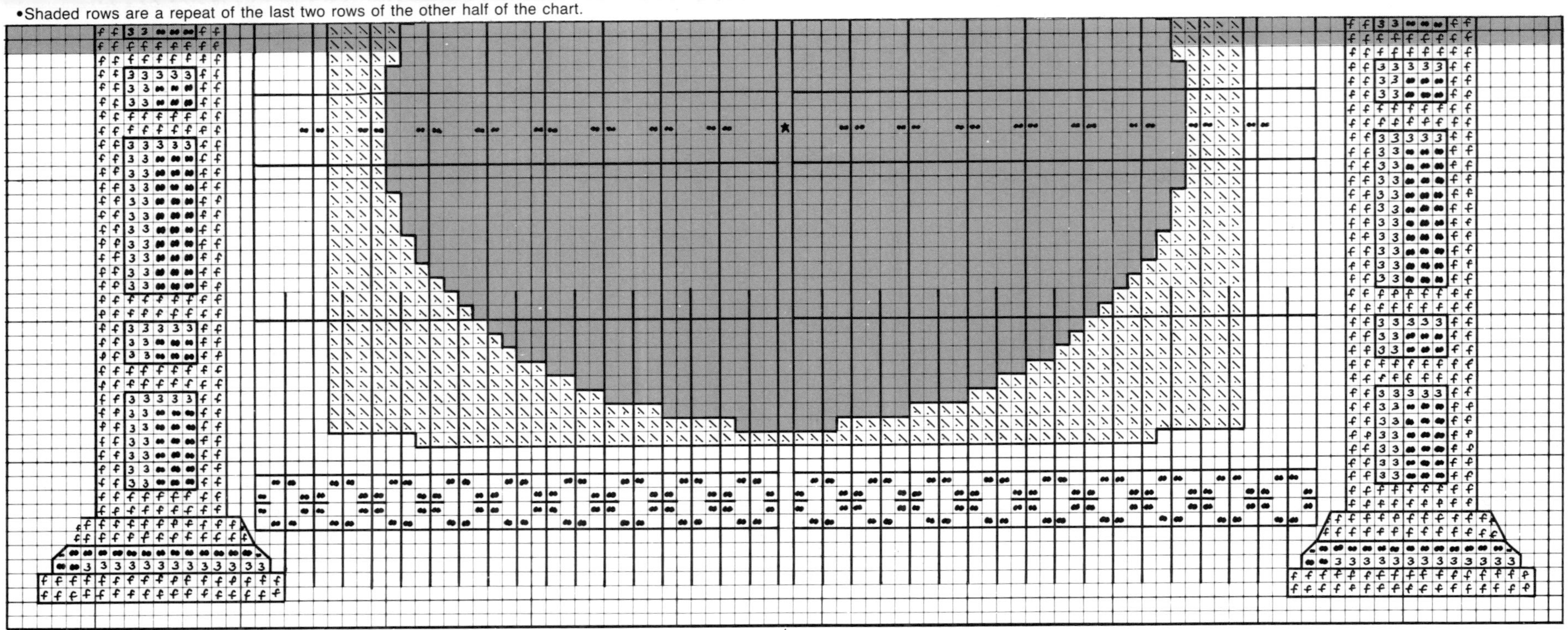

The design area is 103x121; 7″x8-¾″ on 14-count Aida cloth.

The model is stitched on cream 14-count Aida cloth.

Symbol	DMC	Color Description
I	783	christmas gold
◗	310	black
⟍	415	pearl gray
f	414	steel gray, dark
••	413	pewter gray, dark
3	317	pewter gray
h	727	topaz yellow, light
✗	726	topaz yellow
——	783	christmas gold
——	310	black

The angel is backstitched with two strands DMC #783.
The gate posts and gate bars are backstitched with two strands DMC #310.
The wrought iron on the lamps is backstitched with two strands DMC #310.

Instructions for The Temple Gates

This chart can be completed in different ways. If the temple chart is desired as designed above, the stitcher will want to ignore the oval insert and fill in that space with solid DMC #415. Extend the vertical and horizontal iron gate backstitching over the background as graphed.

However, the design can be used as a keepsake for a temple marriage or sealing with the personalizing of the couple's or family names and dates. Also, the phrases "Families Can Be Together Forever" and "Families Are Forever" have been graphed to be inserted in the design.

Three different sizes of inserts are included. The symbol (★) has been included on the Temple Gates chart to help the stitcher center the inserts. Corresponding symbols (★) can be found in the center of the three sizes of ovals. This symbol does not indicate a color but functions as a reference point for positioning each oval in the center of the temple design only. It is recommended that the stitcher draw the outline of the chosen oval on the Temple Gates chart before stitching in order to avoid later stitching errors. The temple background (DMC #415) and the iron gate backstitching (DMC #310) should be filled in to the edge of the drawn-in oval. The stitching inside the oval and the backstitching around it should be done after the Temple Gates stitching area is completed. The size of the oval on this chart corresponds to the two horizontal ovals on pg. 17. (55 sq.x43 sq.) The other two oval sizes will need to be counted out from the (★) symbol and drawn on The Temple Gates Chart by the stitcher.

Families can be Together Forever
Families are Forever

The designs on these two pages can be worked as single projects and mounted in oval hoops, or framed as pictured on the back cover. They also will serve as inserts for the Temple Gates chart of pg. 14-15.

No color coding by specific numbers is given since the stitcher will want to use shades to match the colors in the home or the bride's choice of wedding reception colors. Up to three different colors, each with a darker and lighter shade, can be used in the flowers. Metallic thread or blending filaments can be added for additional sparkle.

The symbols for the flower colors are as follows:

Symbol	Color Description
c	yellow flower center shade
/	light for larger flower
•	dark shade for larger flower
.	light shade for first smaller flower
z	dark shade for first smaller flower

Symbol	Color Description
I	light shade for second smaller flower
▲	dark shade for second smaller flower
x	light green leaf color
Λ	medium green leaf color
o	french knot in medium green color

Use darker shade of flower and leaf colors for all backstitching outlining indicated around corresponding flowers and leaves.

The design area of the two ovals is 63x43; 4-½"x3" on 14-count Aida cloth.
The models are stitched on 14-count Aida cloth.

Personalizing the Temple Gates

The design area of the two horizontal ovals is 55x43; $3^7/_8$"x3" on 14-count Aida cloth.

The design area of the vertical oval is 43x55; 3"x$3^7/_8$" on 14-count Aida cloth.

Instructions for Personalizing The Temple Gates

For the insert using personal names and dates, write out the desired words on a piece of graph paper, using the alphabet printed on pg. 19. Usually one space is left between each letter, and two or three spaces between each word. Some tall and thin letters placed next to each other (i.e. ll, tt, it, li, etc.) can be graphed on opposite sides of the same square.

Then reconstruct the oval on the graph paper and center all lettering, both horizontally and vertically, within the confines of the drawn lines. The number of letters in the names should determine whether the larger or smaller ellipse is used and whether it is placed in a vertical or horizontal position. Work outwards from the * in the center of the oval on the graph paper.

Work the designs in the center of the oval after all the rest of The Temple Gates chart is finished. Backstitch around the edge of the oval last. It is recommended that the letters and oval backstitching be done in two strands of DMC #801, or in any other dominantly darker color.

Floss-Needed Chart

Symbol	Color Description	DMC	Susan Bates	Royal Mouline'	I Feel My Savior's	I Hope They Call	I Love to See	Family Night	Temple Gates
•	white	blanc neige	1	1001	✓	✓	✓	✓	
⅃	antique white	ecru	926	8600				✓	
¢	lavender, dark	209	105	3415			✓		
//	lavender, medium	210	104	3320			✓		
y	lavender	211	108	3410			✓		
o	mahogany, medium	301	349	8315				✓	
◗	black	310	403	1002					✓
$	blue, dark	312	147	4215		✓			
3	pewter gray	317	400	1030					✓
+	steel gray	318	400	1030		✓		✓	
◖	pistachio green, medium	320	216	5015	✓				
7	coral, medium	350	11	2135				✓	
c	peach, medium	353	8	2005	✓	✓		✓	
0	pistachio green, light	368	214	5115	✓				
◥	mahogany, dark	400	351	8325				✓	
••	pewter gray, dark	413	401	1025				✓	✓
f	steel gray, dark	414	399	1020					✓
⋱	pearl gray	415	398	1015				✓	✓
x	hazelnut brown, light	422	373	8710				✓	
ʌ	brown, very light	435	310	8255	✓	✓	✓		
z	tan	436	362	8250			✓	✓	
⧫	tan, light	437	361	8305	✓	✓		✓	
- - - -	shell gray, dark	451	399	1020			✓		
>	shell gray, medium	452	398	1015			✓		
___	avocado green, dark	470	267	5255	✓				
⊂⊃	avocado green, medium	471	266	5245	✓				
N	avocado green, light	472	264	5240	✓				
d	blue green, dark	501	878	5120		✓			
⁄.	sky blue	519	167	4610	✓				
II	drab brown, dark	611	898	5735	✓				
e	drab brown, medium	612	832	8815	✓				
●	beaver gray, dark	645	905	1115		✓			
◨	beaver gray, medium	647	866	1110				✓	
♀	beaver gray, light	648	900	1100				✓	
Γ	antique gold, light	677	292	6130			✓		
E	bittersweet, medium	722	323	7100				✓	
4	topaz	725	306	6215		✓		✓	
⁄•	topaz yellow	726	295	6005					✓
h	topaz yellow, light	727	293	6135	✓				✓
ɛ	tan, very light	738	367	8255	✓			✓	
6	beige	739	366	8240	✓			✓	
..	off white	746	386	6100				✓	
–	peach, light	754	778	8075	✓	✓		✓	
ɔ	pearl gray, light	762	397	1010	✓	✓	✓	✓	
ω	pink, medium	776	36	2110	✓				
⍝	topaz, medium	782	308	6230			✓		
I	christmas gold	783	307	6220			✓		✓
■	brown, dark	801	360	8415	✓	✓	✓	✓	
╲	baby pink	818	23	2610	✓				
▼	beige brown, very dark	838	380	8425		✓			
P	beige brown, dark	839	360	8560		✓			